collections

Hilary Mason

Acknowledgements

The author and publishers would like to thank the teachers and children from the following schools for their enthusiasm, support and creative contributions to the preparation of the classroom displays:

Buckden Primary School; Buckhirst Hill Primary School; Nene Infant School; Peckover Primary School; and Sawtry Infant School.

Special thanks also to: Rob Howard, Curriculum Adviser for Art, Cambridge; Jamie and Sam Coe; Daniel and Carly Heron and Jessica Foote.

Things That Make Us Laugh (page 46)

Shiny Things (page 30)

First published in 1999 by BELAIR PUBLICATIONS LIMITED
Albert House, Apex Business Centre, Boscombe Road, Dunstable, Beds, LU5 4RL

© 1999 Belair on behalf of the author Hilary Mason

Editor: Elizabeth Miles   Design: Jane Conway   Photography: Kelvin Freeman   Cover design: Elaine Baker

Printed in Hong Kong through World Print Limited

ISBN 0 94788 231 6

Contents

Introduction

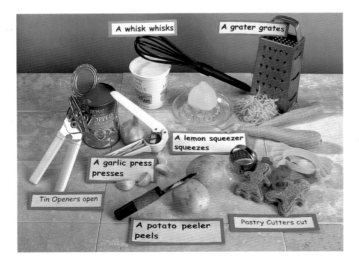

Knowing what to teach is the easy bit. Planning how to create meaningful contexts in which to teach essential skills and processes is sometimes more difficult, and often very time consuming. *Collections* provides those learning contexts.

Each of the following 32 topics uses a collection of readily available objects, such as stones, red things or shiny things, as the stimulus for activities across the curriculum. The activities themselves are designed to help teachers deliver a broad and balanced curriculum.

At the heart of each of the collection topics there is Literacy, Mathematics and Information and Communication Technology (ICT). Beyond that, there are also activities for Science, Humanities and Art and Design.

At the beginning of each collection topic there are suggestions for getting started. This section suggests ways of opening up a discussion with the children about particular objects, and encouraging them to take an active part in building up the collection.

The activities have been designed so that you can get going almost instantly. There is no need to build up a big collection before you embark on a topic. The idea is for the collection to grow as you go along, with the children themselves helping to arrange the displays, and to label and present their work as an integral part of the learning process.

Children learn best when they feel a sense of ownership and engagement with the task. Actively encouraging them to bring things into school to share and work with is therefore an excellent way of capturing their interest at the outset.

Hilary Mason

Winter Things

Getting Started

You will probably begin this topic during the winter, or as winter approaches. Introduce the theme by asking the children about any changes they may have noticed. Talk about the trees, the weather, and animal and bird behaviour. Compare the clothes and shoes they wear in winter with those they wear in summer. What do the children eat and drink, and which sports and leisure activities do they enjoy at different times of the year? Ask the children to bring in to school one item which they use or associate with winter. Add photographs, posters and cards to the collection (see photograph on page 6).

English

- Share stories about the winter, for example *The Snowman* by Raymond Briggs (Puffin), *The Snow Queen* by Hans Christian Andersen (North-South Books) or *Winnie in Winter* by Korky Paul and Valerie Thomas (Oxford University Press). Consider how the characters in the story feel about winter – do the children have similar feelings? Talk about how the illustrations work to reinforce the story's messages.

- Make a list of the winter display collection. Put your list into alphabetical order.

- With the class, talk about all the things you can and can't do in winter (or enjoy/don't enjoy). Make up a class/group poem where each line begins with a refrain such as, 'In the winter we can ...'.

- Try making up some apt and amusing names for the authors of books about winter, such as W Snow, B Lizzard or I C Weather.

- List words and phrases that people use when they are cold, such as freezing, bitter, frost-bitten and chilly. Compare these with words and phrases used for feeling hot.

- Make up alliterative pairs of winter words, for example winter woollies, winter warmers and wet wellies. Display them on a large 'W' outline to use as a winter word bank.

- Write the rest of the story that begins with the sentence, 'There they were again, those strange footprints in the snow.' Collate the group/class stories into a footprint shaped book for others to enjoy.

Mathematics

- Use negative numbers in the context of temperature. Take a series of outdoor temperature readings on freezing days. Compare the temperature readings and put them in order with the lowest first.
  Safety note: Mercury thermometers are not suitable for use in primary schools.

- Investigate winter footwear. How much does a winter shoe weigh compared with a summer sandal? How much more room do boots take up in the cloakroom?

- Use catalogues and magazine advertisements to find the costs of winter clothes. Challenge the children to solve some number and money problems. For example, estimate and then find how much you would need to spend on a new winter coat, hat and scarf.

Information and Communication Technology

- Use a concept keyboard and overlays. Ask the children to match pictures of clothes and other winter items, such as skis, with the correct word. Help the children to make up some of their own for a friend to try.

- Use a computer to make a weather chart to record weekly weather. You could print out several and use them to monitor the weather over a month or a term.

Science

- Demonstrate to the children how to use a thermometer safely and accurately. Encourage them to explore how a thermometer reading changes when they hold it in their hand, put it near a warm radiator or run it under a cold tap.

- Ask the children to think about which materials they use for keeping warm in winter. Test those materials by wrapping them around a container of warm water to find out which keeps the container warm the longest. Record the temperature of the water at regular intervals.

- Investigate which materials are best for keeping people dry on rainy days in winter. Give the children a range of materials (some waterproof, some not). Drop water on to the materials. Which ones let the water through? Was it a fair test?

Humanities

- Consider the effects of winter on people and their surroundings. How does winter affect what people do in terms of food, clothes and leisure? What influence does winter have on their surroundings, including their home, school, local landscape, animals, roads and so on?

- Go for a walk around the school grounds and the area immediately outside the school gates. Draw a map to show the likely trouble spots where visitors will need to be careful during bad weather, for example slopes that may become icy, dips and pot holes that could fill with water, areas around trees that could get slippery.

Art and Design

- Make large, mixed-media wall collages of 'winter landscapes' or 'having fun in the snow' (see photographs on page 5 and above).

- Explore the use of a print roller by printing winter tree silhouettes (see photograph, below).

- Which colours do the children consider to be cold? Why? How do they feel about them? Practise mixing cold colours and use them to make winter patterns, for example cloud or frost and icicle shapes, diagonal lines, or spatter printing to represent rain falling. Use some of your patterned sheets to make lettering for titles, labels and so on.

Summer Things

Getting Started

You could begin by taking the children on a summer walk and talking about seasonal changes. Draw their attention to the signs of summer: birds singing, summer gardens in bloom, insects buzzing and shop-window displays. Discuss what is most enjoyable about summer and start to collect items associated with favourite summer pastimes and summer holidays for display (see photograph, right).

English

- List as many summer things as you can think of. Ask the children to incorporate some or all of these into a composite picture. Add labels or short captions.

- Add adjectives to embellish your summer things vocabulary bank, for example 'bright red bucket and spade', 'cool, cotton shorts' and 'icy cold drinks'. Try the same idea with similes or alliteration, for example 'fruit drinks like a refreshing stream' or 'plastic plates please'.

- Compile a recipe book of summer or picnic foods. Can the children think up warm, sunny names for their favourite food and drink?

- Look at a selection of holiday postcards. Discuss the features, such as a picture on one side and a blank space on the reverse to write in, a space or lines for the address and an outline indicating where to stick a stamp. Give the children plain postcards and ask them to design a postcard of a favourite summer place, write a simple message on the back and fill in their home address.

Mathematics

- Classify and chart your summer collection into clothes, foods and leisure activities.

- Decorate paper picnic plates with repeated geometric shapes (see photograph, below).

- Collect data on favourite places to visit, holiday destinations or leisure activities. How many people like swimming or lying on the beach best?

- Fill up a picnic box. You are allowed to choose three things from this list: sandwiches, savoury rolls, pizza slice, fruit or jam tarts. Can you make up five different picnic boxes?

- Use holiday brochures to investigate the cost of holidays. How much would it cost two adults and two children to stay in the cheapest/most expensive hotel in a chosen location?

Information and Communication Technology

- Use a word processor to practise writing your name and address. Print them out and make them into luggage or clothes labels.

- Compose a short e-mail message to a friend or parent inviting them to your school's summer fair.

- Find out about the potential dangers of over-exposing the skin to the sun. Make a poster or information sheet about harmful rays, recommended clothing (sunhats and long-sleeved shirts) and sun-screen lotions, to encourage people to protect themselves.

Science

- Take the children into the playground on a cloudy day in summer to identify the changes that occur when the sun goes behind a cloud. Ask them to decide (without looking at the sun) when it goes behind a cloud and when it re-emerges. How they can tell? Record their suggestions.
Safety note: Warn children NEVER to look directly at the sun. Blindness can result.

- Set up a shadow stick and ask the children to measure and record the length of the shadow at different times of the day. Record the results in a table and present them as a bar graph. Discuss the data.

- Ask the children to consider ways of keeping things cold in hot weather, for example how to keep drinks cold in a picnic basket. Investigate different wrappings, such as aluminium foil, bubble wrap and sponge, by placing each one around an ice cube. Identify which is the most effective in stopping the ice cube from melting. Make a table of your results.

Humanities

- Record how many sunny days there are over a week, month or term. Older or more able children could extend this to a fuller record of weather conditions and then analyse the data.

- Plot summer recreational amenities, such as the swimming pool, leisure centre or park, on a local map. On the map, draw arrows to these facilities and illustrate them with an appropriate symbol or 3D model and key.

Art and Design

- Create mixed-media sand and water collages of summer or beach scenes. Think carefully about the most suitable colours, textures and materials (see photograph, right).

- Investigate warm colours. Which colours make the children think of the summer? Practise mixing warm colours and use them to paint summer patterns.

- Use ink or acrylic paint to print pattern designs on fabric to make a tablecloth or spread for a picnic. Which colours would mix well to produce bright summer colours?

- Prepare and make summer picnic food and drinks, and invite friends from another class to share them. Try sandwiches and buns, or make ice-lollies from different flavoured fruit juices.

Natural Things

our pastel pictures of natural things in the park

Getting Started

The items in your final display collection will, to some extent, depend on the season, but you are bound to find some dried grasses, flower seed-heads, or twigs, stones and feathers around the school. Promote curiosity by adding an item to your starter collection which is 'unnatural' or manufactured such as a spoon or a felt-tip pen. Who can spot the odd one out? Try to take the children on a woodland walk or nature trail and discuss the importance of taking care of the environment (see Humanities, page 11).

English

- Share some stories with the children about the natural environment, for example *One World* by Michael Foreman (Red Fox); *Bringing the Rain to Kapiti Plain* by Verna Aardema (Macmillan); and *Oi! Get off our Train* by John Burningham (Red Fox). Discuss and list the messages and key themes in the stories. Which endangered animals are shown in John Burningham's book?

- To develop listening skills, take the children outside for a 'sound walk'. Ask them to stand absolutely still with their eyes closed and listen carefully to the sounds around them. Can they describe and identify the sounds they hear? You could make a picture chart of these sounds – which were made by people, birds or animals, and which were made by machines or other 'unnatural' things?

- Write a letter to an environmental organisation asking if they will help you set up a conservation area in your school grounds. The children may want to ask for financial help or general advice about types of plants or how to maintain a pond.

Mathematics

- Make some family number trees and ask the children to work out the number facts. Provide additional branches for the children to continue the number sequence.

- Use the natural objects as a stimulus for number problems. Examples: If one flower has 5 petals how many petals do 2, 3 and 4 flowers have? If a seed-head contains 100 seeds how many seeds do 2 seed-heads have? Challenge the children to make up some of their own number problems using the display collection and to use their ideas to make a natural numbers quiz sheet.

Family number trees

Information and Communication Technology

- Use a computer to design a poster advertising a new nature trail or woodland walk. Highlight the opening hours, location and any special features, such as observation areas. Practise changing the font size and style to emphasise different sorts of information and include some appropriate clip art on screen.

- Use the Internet to find out about environmental organisations and nature clubs which the children may like to join. Help them to send an e-mail to a chosen organisation asking for further details.

Science

- Make careful observational drawings of flowers, seeds or dried grasses. Look at the items under a magnifier and record what you see. Use reference sources to identify and label the plants.

Can you spot the objects that don't belong in our natural things picture ?

- Present the children with a variety of natural and manufactured items: twigs, bones, pine cones, paper, glass and plastic. Sort them into natural/manufactured sets. Discuss how the manufactured items, such as paper and glass, may have been made out of natural materials. Use secondary sources to find out how these items are made.

Humanities

- Take the children on a walk in the local park or wood. Look for unnatural or manufactured items in the natural environment, such as litter bins, a park bench or statue. A walk through a town in search of natural items can also be interesting and will help children to express their views on the attractive and unattractive features of an environment made by people. Ask them to consider how the quality of each environment can be sustained and improved.

Art and Design

- Make a mixed-media collage or large wall frieze of a natural scene such as a park or woodland. Hide some manufactured items in the picture and ask if anyone can spot the 'odd ones out'. (See display photograph, above.)

- Explore the effects of printing and painting with feathers. (Use paint-filled sponges to apply the paint to the feathers.) Experiment with the effects of using different hand movements (flicking, swirling, pressing and twisting) to make interesting patterns. Complete the effect by attaching the feathers to the finished design.

- Construct 'natural' sculptures or mobiles from items such as twigs, stones, feathers and shells.

- Use a variety of dried grasses, twigs, stems and seed-heads to create natural weavings.

- Use pastel crayons to create pictures of a woodland or park which the children may have visited. Ask them to include at least five of the natural things in their picture (see photograph on page 10).

House Plants

Getting Started

Start off your plant display by collecting as many house plants as you can spare from home or around the school. Try to include plants of various sizes, with different shaped leaves and leaf markings, and some with flowers. It is also useful to have at least a few interesting plant pots to add to the display. Ask the children to bring in a plant from home to add to the starter collection. Encourage them to find out the name of the plant and write it down (or ask an adult to write it for them).

English

- Compile a class catalogue of your house plants collection. Draw a picture of each plant and add a caption giving the name of the plant and the owner, for example 'This is a cheese plant. It belongs to Winston's Grandma'. Put the catalogue into alphabetical order by plant name.

- Some people believe that you should talk to your plants to help them grow. What sort of things would the children say to their plants? Plan imaginary conversations and display them in speech bubbles or as a two-frame picture and caption sequence.

- Write a story about a house plant that grew and grew. You could extend this idea into an indoor version of *Jack and the Beanstalk*, for example 'Jess and the Spider Plant' or 'Charlie and the Cheese Plant'.

Mathematics

- Order your house plants from shortest to tallest. Estimate and measure the height of each plant using standard or non-standard units.

- Make up some plant mathematics problems for a friend to solve. For example: If a plant grows 3 centimetres a month, how much will it grow in 2, 3 and 6 months, and in a year? If a spider plant has 5 baby plants in 6 months how many will it have in 2 years?

- Measure what capacity of water a plant needs over 1–2 weeks. Chart which plant needed the most and least water.

Information and Communication Technology

- Use a word processor to write a set of instructions for potting a new plant. Each stage of the instructions should start on a new line. Will the children use numbers or bullet points to order the instructions?

- Use a computer to design an advertisement for a garden centre or florist's shop specialising in house plants (see photograph, left). Children should work in pairs or small groups to research this kind of advertisement in their local directory. Can they devise an apt name for the shop?

Science

- What do the children think seeds need in order to grow? Plant some fast-growing seeds, such as broad beans, sunflower or marrow seeds, in compost. Discuss and record the changes in root, shoot and leaf growth at regular intervals and consolidate knowledge of the names of plant parts as the seedlings grow. Make a chart to record daily observations.

- Present the children with a wilting house plant and ask them to suggest ideas for reviving it. Can they devise a test to identify the importance of water in the life of a plant?

- Show the children a plant that has grown too large for its pot. Remove it and look carefully at the roots. Ask the children why they think it needs re-potting. Compare the roots with those of seedlings. What similarities and differences can they see?

- Ask the children to summarise what they have found out about leaves, stems and roots by drawing and labelling a plant that is in good conditions for growth and one in conditions that will hinder growth.

Humanities

- Which areas of the indoor school environment could be made to look more cheerful by the addition of some house plants? Children could mark these areas on a plan of the school.

- Think about why people often give plants to friends who are feeling fed up or unwell.

Art and Design

- Draw still-life pastel pictures of house plants (see photograph, above).

- Design and make a pot for a house plant. Ask the children about the important features they should consider, for example water-proofing and drainage.

- Make a decorative name label for a particular house plant.

- Practise colour mixing different shades of green to make a green colour chart. Use these shades of green in mixed-media collage pictures of house plants, or for designing a wrapping paper that a florist might use.

Fruit

Getting Started

Take a few pieces of fruit into school, including some slightly more exotic ones such as mango, kiwi, guava, lychee, and some dried fruit such as currants, apricots and sultanas. Ask the children to name as many different fruits as they can. Do they know which countries the fruits come from? When do the children enjoy eating fruit?

English

- Read and talk about the story, *Oliver's Fruit Salad* by Vivian French (Hodder Children's Books). Ask the children to describe the different fruit salad items. Encourage them to add as much detail as possible. Focus on each of the senses, for example 'it is red/heart-shaped/round', 'it smells like ...', 'it sounds crunchy ...'. Make a zig-zag book showing how to prepare a fruit salad.

- Make a class list of fruit names. Help the children to think up some alliterative adjectives to go with each fruit, for example bendy banana, luscious lemon and mighty mango. Ask the children to draw and write captions using these descriptions, and combine them into a wall frieze.

- Compile a book of fruit riddles. On one page write some clue descriptions of a particular fruit, for example 'I am yellow/curved/sometimes a bit spotty'. Reveal the answer on the next page. Some children could try making up more cryptic clues, for example 'My name is a colour' or 'I am very bitter but you like me in squash'.

Mathematics

- On a timeline of the children's day show when they eat fruit, or use clock faces and ask them to draw the fruits they eat at particular times, for example breakfast, at playtime and for lunch.

- Ask the children to investigate how many different ways a fruit, such as an apple or an orange, can be shared equally between 2, 3 and 4 people. Chart the results.

- Investigate which fruits in your collection weigh the most and least. How many lemons does it take to balance, for example, 4 apples or 0.5 kilograms of grapes? Try other comparisons using standard or non-standard measures.

Information and Communication Technology

- Help the children to use a spreadsheet to show the results of a class survey of favourite fruits.

- Use a word processing program to print a poster advertising a special fruit promotion day at your school. You could use the paint/draw or a clip art facility to add images to the design, or print out the text and ask the children to illustrate it by hand.

Science

- Present the children with a collection of seeds and fruits of different shapes, sizes and colours, for example tomato, apple, mango, grape and avocado. Discuss and record how fruit grows. Look at pictures of plants in flower and with fruit, such as apples, plums and horse chestnuts, and explain that the fruits contain the seeds which are produced from the flowers.

- Cut open a variety of fruits and make close observational drawings. Use magnifiers to look again at the inside of the fruit and make another drawing. Display as comparative pairs of labelled drawings.

- Find out and discuss why fruit is an essential part of a healthy diet. Record which fruits are particularly high in vitamins and fibre. Display information on a poster entitled, 'Apples are good for us because ...'. Repeat for other fruits.

Humanities

- Visit your local market, or supermarket. Find out which of the fruits are grown in your own country and which come from overseas. Locate these on a world map.

- Find out more about the countries where some of your fruits are grown, for example where do most bananas come from? How do they get from these countries into our shops? Produce some 'Going Bananas' fact sheets to record your findings.

Art and Design

- Use a range of fabrics and materials to make collage pictures of fruits. Add stitched detail (see display photograph on page 14).

- Make a fruit salad. As part of the planning process, first list the fruits and equipment you will need. Consider its appearance, the most pleasing colours, the cost, and whether each fruit should be peeled, sliced, diced or grated.

- Look at the *Four Seasons* paintings by artist Giuseppe Archimboldo (1527–93) in which he represented the four stages of adult life through portraits consisting of different seasonal fruits and vegetables. Ask the children to cut out fruits from magazines to create 'fruity face' portraits, or use real fruits to create 3D faces (see photographs, above and left).

Shells

Getting Started

You will probably have a collection of at least a few shells in school to start off the display. Many children will have shells they have brought back from the seaside; others may have large conch shells, given to them as souvenirs. Ask the children to bring the shells in to add to the collection. Remember to talk about other types of shells, for example tortoise, turtle and snail shells.

English

- Share stories about the seaside. A very popular read is *Sally and the Limpet* by Simon Jones (Walker Books). Discuss the sorts of creatures and plants that live in seawater, including shellfish.

- Use a large shell as a device for encouraging children to take turns during speaking and listening activities – only the person holding the shell is allowed to speak.

- Explore the 'ell' rime. What other words or onsets can the children think of that rhyme with 'shell'? Answers might include bell, fell, sell, tell, yell and well. Encourage them to discriminate, read and spell words ending in 'ell'.

- Have fun with tongue-twisters. Begin with the classic 'She sells sea shells on the sea shore'. Who can keep going the longest without getting in a muddle? Ask the children to write another line or two, for example 'She sings shell songs sitting in the sun'. The children could draw and write the caption for the extended version.

- Write some imaginative sentences based on the question: What did the shell tell?

Mathematics

- Design and play a simple number game based on a snail-shaped board. Roll a die and move that number of spaces or use two dice and add the numbers, then move. Or, only move when the number thrown is odd or even. Some children could add other dimensions to the game, such as bonuses and forfeits about solving mental mathematics or number problems.

- Use collections of shells to make estimates of numbers. Ask the children to estimate a number of shells up to about 30. Count the shells to find the correct number.

- Estimate and weigh the different shells in your collection using standard or non-standard units. Put them in order according to their weight, starting with the lightest.

Information and Communication Technology

- Use a CD-ROM or the Internet to find out more about animals or molluscs that live inside a shell.

- Set up a database of information to record what you find out about your chosen animal.

Science

- Observe an invertebrate, such as a snail, and compare its body with that of a human. Research and report on how the bodies of animals without bony skeletons are supported.

- Which animals or molluscs can the children name that live inside a shell? Why do they think creatures such as snails, turtles, crabs and tortoises have a hard shell? Using research material, work in groups to find out about one of these animals or molluscs. What do they eat? Where do they lay their eggs? How long do they take to hatch? Present findings as an illustrated information booklet.

Snail Shell Patterns

Art and Design

- Look at a picture of a turtle, tortoise or snail (or look at the real thing if you can). Focus on the markings and patterns. Try replicating these on Plasticine or clay models.

- Use gold and silver crayons or pens to make snail shell patterns, and let the children mount their own pictures on brown paper (see photograph, left).

- Make a large, class wall frieze or collage based on a seaside or shell story you have enjoyed together. For example, *The Seashell Song* by Susie Jenkin-Pearce (Red Fox) or *Sally and the Limpet* by Simon Jones. (See photograph on page 16.)

- Make spiral or shell mobiles.

Skulls and Bones

Getting Started

Ideally, your school will already have a small collection of skulls and bones, or you may have or be able to borrow a full-size skeleton. If not, start by asking the children to explore their own bones. Where are the ribs? Are they hard or soft? How many can they feel? Ask the children to take off their shoes and socks and feel the bones in their feet and hands (most of the skeleton's bones are found in the hands, wrists, feet and ankles). Can the children name any bones in the body (skull, backbone, shoulder blade and so on)?

English

- Look at the words 'skeleton' and 'skull'. Notice how they both start with the initial consonant blend 'sk'. Write other 'sk' words on bone shapes and display them as a skeleton mobile (skin, skates, sketch, skip). Try adding adjectives or verbs in front of the word 'skeleton' to make alliterative phrases, such as skinny/skipping/skating skeleton.

- Talk about the wishbone idea. Write about something you would wish for, or a wish that actually came true.

- There are lots of sayings and adages about bones. Try to remember some, or ask other people. Examples: lazy bones, down to the bare bones, bone idle. Write and illustrate these sayings, and collate them into a bone-shaped class book. Think of a fun and appropriate title, for example *The Numb Skull Book*.

Mathematics

- Use your fingers to help learn the 9 times tables. Spread out your hands and imagine your fingers (including thumbs) are numbered 1 to 10 from left to right. To work out 9 x 4 bend down your fourth finger. Then count the fingers to the left (3) and the fingers to the right (6). The answer is 36.

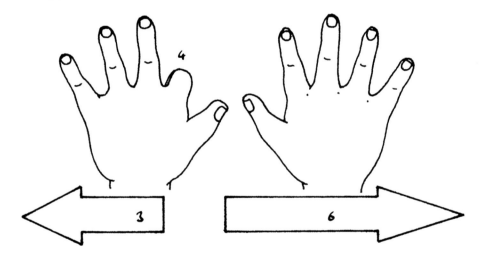

- Measure some of the bones in your collection. Record these measurements and add the labels to your collection. What is the best way of measuring the skull?

- Survey head, arm or leg measurements in your class. Do the tallest people always have the longest legs? Are adults' heads larger than children's heads? Do boys have longer arms than girls? Present the results as tables, bar charts or pictograms, and discuss what the data shows.

Information and Communication Technology

- Make a database of class bone measurements; for example, hands, feet, the distance from thigh to knee. The database fields could be previously agreed with the class; for example, name, date, measurements. Update the database once every term and record any changes.

- Use secondary resource material such as a CD-ROM or the Internet to research amazing facts about bones. Print out and display the information in different font sizes and styles (see photograph on page 19).

Science

- Ask the children to find out the names and locate the major bones in the human skeleton, for example skull, spine, ribs and so on. Add the labels to your skeleton model or to a large outline diagram of the human body. Practise removing and replacing the labels to match the correct bones.

- Look at the variety of bones in your classroom collection and ask the children to describe their properties, for example whether they are hard, brittle, strong, smooth or rough. If possible display X-rays of human bones to show that although bones are strong they do break.

- Use secondary sources to find out how the bodies of animals without bony skeletons are supported. The information should be recorded and shared with the rest of the class.

- Find out and record what the body needs to maintain healthy bones.

Art and Design

- Make moving skeletons using string or card levers and drinking straws for the bones (see diagrams, right).

- Make close observational drawings of skulls and bones (see photograph, above).

- Make some 'fossils' of your own by imprinting snail shells, leaves or small bones into Plasticine or clay. These can be filled with plaster to create moulds of each impression.

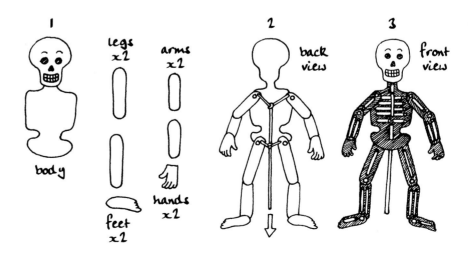

Stones

Getting Started

An interesting way of launching a topic on stones is to show the children one stone and begin a discussion about it. Any stone will work as a starter – one you pick up in the garden on the way to school, a special gem stone, a stone with a hole in it or a polished stone. Ask the children to describe the stone to you. Where do they think it has come from? What words can they think of to describe the colours, texture and shape?

Consider with the children all the places where they have seen stones, and what they are used for. Ask them to collect some interesting stones and bring them into school for your collection and to use for practical activities. Try to make sure you include a range of different sized stones and pebbles, and, if possible, some fossils.

English

- Use stones to practise initial letter sounds by making 3D letters formed from different sorts of stones. These could be made into an alphabet wall frieze.

- Use pebbles as full stops when practising sentence construction.

- Use a stone as a device for encouraging children to take turns during speaking and listening activities. For example, only the person holding the stone is allowed to speak or ask a question.

- Ask the children to select three stones and make up riddles about each of them, for example 'I am speckled grey. My surface is smooth. You can see through a part of me.' Can others work out which stone is being described?

Mathematics

- How many classroom objects such as building bricks, wooden cubes or beads does it take to balance one particular stone? Record the results in a chart.

- Can the children order the stones from smallest to largest or heaviest to lightest?

- Use pebbles or small stones to practise number bonds and number facts to 10, 20 and 30. Pose problems such as 'If I have 10 stones and I take 2 away, how many will I have left?'

- Use round stones to play a simple board game based on the hop-scotch idea. Place two stones on the number squares – how much do the squares add up to?

Information and Communication Technology

- Make up a story about a magic stone. Use a word processor to draft, edit and print out the story.

- Use a CD-ROM information resource or the Internet to find out about the Stone Age or Stonehenge.

- Use secondary sources such as CD-ROMs to find out about fossils. What are they? How are they formed? How old might they be? Record your findings as a short picture and text book for a younger child.

Science

- Take the children outside into the school grounds or local park to look for evidence of the sorts of creatures that live under stones. Find out more about these living things. Why do they like to be under stones?

  Note: Children need to be reminded that they must not disturb the animals they find under the stones.

- Give the children a collection of rocks and stones to observe and group according to their characteristics: for example texture, shape, size, appearance, arrangement of particles or colour. Ask the children to select a criterion for grouping their rocks and to identify what it is with a label.

- Test the permeability of the stones in your display collection by dropping small quantities of water on to them and observing whether it stays on the surface or permeates through the stone.

Humanities

- Go out into your local environment to look for evidence of how rocks and different types of stone have been used in buildings, for pavements, as decoration and in monuments.

- Older or more able children could research the rock cycle and then make a picture and caption sequence of the story of a rock – from a mountain boulder to a small stone or pebble in a river.

Art and Design

- Make fantastical stone creatures. Try gluing some oddly-shaped stones together and painting or sticking on fabric claws, feathers, wings and other features (see photograph, left).

- Print with different shaped stones to make some special wrapping paper.

- Make a paperweight as a present. Decorate a smooth stone – how can you stop the decoration from coming off on hands or important papers?

- Make and decorate a treasure box to hold three special stones and add a lid.

- Make 3D models of creatures which live under stones.

Treasures

Getting Started

What do the children understand by the word 'treasure'? Show them something which is special to you. Talk to them about why it is of special significance and why you treasure it so much – perhaps you have had it since you were a child or you bought it on a special holiday. Ask the children about the kinds of things they treasure, which might include foreign coins, letters from a pen friend, a soft toy, sporting trophies or a photograph. Make a class collection of the children's treasures.

English

- Ask the children to introduce their personal treasure to the rest of the class. Encourage them to say at least one sentence about it. Help the class to compile a series of questions to ask the owner to find out more about the particular treasure. For example: Where did you get your treasure? Why is it so special to you? How do you keep it safe?

- Ask the children to write a sentence about why their treasured item is so special. Add these descriptions to the display.

- Ask the children to work in pairs to write a sentence about something they treasure about themselves, for example their teeth, sense of humour or a favourite article of clothing they wear. Next, ask them to write a sentence about something that is special about their partner. Discuss and compare the two observations.

- Tell the children some real-life stories about treasure and artefacts that have been found on the sea-bed, in caves or tombs, such as the *Mary Rose* recovery or the opening of Tutankhamun's tomb. Can the children act out or write a story about finding missing treasure?

- Write acrostic poems from the word 'TREASURES' or use the letters from a child's own special object, such as 'COINS' OR 'TEDDY'.

- Compile a class or group picture book or catalogue with a repetitive, minimal text refrain such as 'My ... is/are special because ...'. Can the children think of a good idea for the title and front cover illustration?

Mathematics

- Use some or all of your special things to practise number facts and bonds; for example: How many special things have they collected altogether? How many would there be if 2, 5 or 10 people took their treasure home tonight? How many would there be if only half as many people had brought in their special things? Help the children to make up more questions to ask each other.

- Chart on a class timeline how long children have had their special treasures (or the date they started collecting them). The children may have to check dates with parents or carers.

- Practise simple co-ordinates by playing a treasure hunt game with the children's own collected treasures.

Information and Communication Technology

- Use a tape recorder and microphone to interview each other about your special treasure.

- Use the computer to make some invitations to invite parents, or another class, to view and hear a short talk on your treasures collection.

- Keep an inventory of who brought in which special things by making a simple database. Enter data such as name, item brought in, date brought in and date taken home.

- The children could use a disposable camera to photograph their special treasures. Use copies of the photographs as part of the inventory activity or co-ordinates game.

Humanities

- Many of the children's parents, grandparents or other known members of the community will have treasured collections of things such as war memorabilia, old photographs and souvenirs. Invite one or two of them in to share their feelings and stories about their special things.

- Find out about the special things that were treasured by ancient civilisations, such as the Egyptians, Greeks or Vikings. What sorts of treasures did the pharaohs have buried in their pyramids, for example?

- Find out about the special things involved in celebrations such as Diwali (lights, new clothes), Hanukkah (the menorah, dreidel, presents) or Chinese New Year (lanterns, red streamers, special money). What is the history and the story behind these treasures?

Art and Design

- Make and decorate a container or box to keep your treasured item safe or to give as a present for somebody you know well (see photograph, right).

- Collage a 'Treasures under the Sea' frieze to display aspects of your own treasure story or a story you have read (see photograph on page 22).

- Design and make an alarm, incorporating an electrical circuit to keep treasures safe. Draw and label design ideas first. Will they use a buzzer or flashing light? What sort of switch will activate the alarm?

Broken Things

Getting Started

Ask the children to bring in something from home which is broken. Talk about the sorts of things they might bring, to ensure that the collection includes a range of broken items, such as toys, gadgets, radios, game-box lids, clocks, pots and if possible something larger, like a bicycle.

As the children bring their broken things into school, ask them to identify and describe what they think is wrong with them and why they don't work anymore. Ask questions and talk about what we do with things that are broken. For example: Who fixes things in their house? Where do they take things to be repaired?

English

- Talk or write about an event when something you really liked was broken, or the consequences of when you broke something belonging to someone else.

- Turn your display into a mini-repair shop. Think up a name for it and a few words to sum up the service it offers, such as 'Fix Its – we mend anything'.

- Role-play customer and repairer. Help the children to think about the sorts of information that must be exchanged, for example an explanation of the problems, how long the repairer thinks it will take to mend and how much the work will cost. Practise asking and answering questions clearly and politely.

- Make a picture or word list of the items waiting to be repaired in your workshop. Put the list into alphabetical order.

- Help the children to write some questions about your broken things focusing on 'wh' words. For example: What is wrong with this (lamp/sewing machine, etc.)? When was it broken? Where shall we take it to be repaired? Why do we want to mend it?

- Make up a circle story or class poem about one of the broken objects in your display collection. Themes could be an old broken clock or a sewing machine that is repaired and then makes magical garments. Write and illustrate the stories.

Mathematics

- Create mathematical problems using the broken items in the collection. For example: What time did the broken clock stop? What time would it have been 1 hour earlier or 30 minutes later?

- If it takes one week from now to fix a bicycle, what will the date be when it is ready for collection?

- Estimate how much thread will be needed to sew teddy's ear back on. How much thread would you need to sew on two new ears?

Information and Communication Technology

- Compile a class book of instructions for fixing things. Make sure the repair method is fairly simple, for example sticking a page back into a book, mending a game-box lid or sewing on a button. The children should use a recognised, regular format such as one line (perhaps starting with a bullet point) for each stage of the instructions.

- Use a word processing and clip art package to design a price list or notice to display in the shop window of 'Rose's bicycle repair shop'.

Humanities

- Try to visit a garage, workshop or bicycle repair shop or invite a mechanic, cobbler or carpenter into school to talk to the children. Ask the children to prepare a list of questions to ask.

- Use a local directory or newspaper advertisements to find out where the broken things in your collection, or items such as cars, bicycles or electrical goods, can be repaired in your area. Can the children locate these on a local map?

- Consider and list alternative uses for the broken items in your collection. Can any of them be recycled into other useful things? Could any of the components, such as screws, tubes and cables, be kept as spare parts?

Art and Design

- Try printing a picture or create a collage with the screws, nuts, threads, bolts or off-cuts of wood from broken items.

- Make a close observational drawing of an item from the display collection or the components found in one of the broken things.

- Ask the children to select broken items from the display collection to create an interesting still-life composition to sketch or paint.

Tools

A whisk whisks

A grater grates

A lemon squeezer squeezes

A garlic press presses

Tin Openers open

A potato peeler peels

Pastry Cutters cut

Getting Started

If possible bring into school some tools you may have at home, such as a hammer, screwdriver, pliers and paintbrush. Try to include some kitchen tools, such as a cheese grater, garlic press or food whisk. Show the tools to the children and talk about how they help us to mend, fix and make things more easily. What other sorts of tools can the children name? Who might use them?

English

- Write poetry inspired by the sounds tools make or their functions. Display your poems on outline tool shapes (see display photograph on page 27).

- Explore the long 'oo' sound in 'tools'. Brainstorm and list words the children know, for example food, boots, broom, moon and so on. Ask the children to make a labelled drawing, or write an illustrated story, showing themselves on the moon with some of the 'oo' things they have identified.

- Enjoy reading some of the ever popular 'Happy Families' books by Allan Ahlberg (Puffin Books), for example *Mrs Plug the Plumber, Miss Brick the Builder's Baby* or *Mrs Lather's Laundry,* with the children. Discuss the characters' jobs, what tasks were involved and what tools and equipment they used to help them. Create some new additions to the Ahlberg 'Happy Families' books based on tools, for example Ms Brush the Decorator, Mr Needle the Tailor and Master Whisk the Apprentice Chef. Write a day in the life of these new characters.

- Discuss the different names for tools or kitchen implements and show how many of their names are linked to the job they do, such as a saw saws and a grater grates. Establish that the naming words for tools often come from the verbs describing what they do or vice versa, for example sand/sander, scrape/scraper. Ask the children to find other examples. (See photograph, above.)

Mathematics

- Brainstorm, collect and make a picture chart of as many tools as you can think of that help us with mathematics, such as rulers, tapes, trundle wheels, calculators and computers. Ask the children to sort the mathematics tools into sets, such as those used for counting, adding, measuring length, capacity, weight and time.

- Can the children select and use the appropriate mathematical equipment to carry out investigations, for example to measure the hall or playground, or find out about volume?

- Talk about how useful a calculator can be as a tool for handling big numbers or complex problems, as well as for checking answers. Set some calculator challenges: ask the children to count from zero in 2s, 3s, 5s, 10s and 100s and count backwards beyond zero; convert fractions to decimals (divide the numerator by the denominator), check multiplication sums or reinforce tables.

Information and Communication Technology

- Consider and list all the ways in which computers and information technology help us with communications, work and pleasure (telephone, Internet, CDs and so on). Print out the list and illustrate it to add to your tools display.

- Provide opportunities for children to use the tools listed for purposes of communication, work and pleasure. Set up a spreadsheet and ask the children to access and update the file over a term showing when they have used each item and for what purpose.

Science

- Identify movement words that are related to the use of tools, for example twisting, pushing, pulling, turning, driving, rolling, hitting and rotating. Talk about the types of movement required for the tools in the display collection.

- Look at the different forces required to work the hand tools in your classroom collection. Challenge the children to identify and sort which tools work by using both a pushing and pulling motion, such as a saw, those which only require a push, such as a garlic press and those that require a pull, such as a claw hammer.

- Help the children to recognise the hazards and risks of working with tools. Look carefully at each tool and consider why it is important to take care when using it. Ask the children to design a classroom poster explaining the correct use of tools.

Art and Design

- Make close observational drawings of the various tools in your collection.

- Make some carefully observed 3D models of the tools from Plasticine. Use PVA glue to harden them and mount them on shiny card (see display photograph, above).

- Allow the children to use the tools and appropriate materials to explore and practise skills such as hammering, sawing and driving screws into wood.

- Provide opportunities for cooking and baking so that the children can use a variety of kitchen tools such as hand whisks, rolling pins and cutters.

- Make interesting Plasticine or clay slab impressions of the patterns made from tools. For example, serrated edges of saws, the pattern created by a Pozidrive screwdriver, a grater or ball/claw hammer indentations.

Old Things

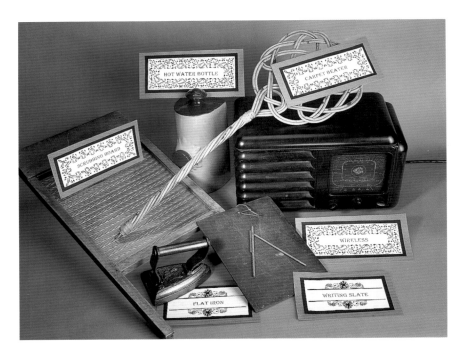

Getting Started

What do the children understand by the term 'old things'? As well as the more obvious historical items they may, for example, include in their definitions things they have had for a while and no longer use, such as toys or clothes. Decide together what sorts of objects and artefacts you will include in your old things collection, and review your decisions as you go along. Ask the children to bring in old things from home, including books, domestic appliances, artefacts or clothes from a past era.

English

- Let the children take turns to choose an object from your collection as a starting point for a circle story. Whoever chooses the object begins the story, then take turns to add something such as a word, sentence or character. Record some of the stories.

- Make a phonic wheel to discriminate between onset and rime in spelling using the letter string 'old'. Change the onset to the word by adding consonants b, c, f, g, h, s and t to the rime (see right).

- Select an item from your collection for the children to focus on more closely. Ask them to describe a particular 'old thing', either verbally or in writing. Encourage the use of comparative and descriptive language, and the use of adjectives and similes – what does the shape, colour and texture remind them of?

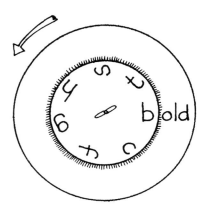

Phonic wheel

Mathematics

- Record the weights and heights of some of your old things – which are the heaviest and lightest? Were the children surprised by any of the measurements (for example, an old flat iron is not very tall, but it is heavy, while Dad's old rain boots are tall but quite light)? Add these findings to the display.

- Imagine you are having a second-hand sale of your old things. Work out some price tags for them and use these to practise money and change work.

- Look at dates printed on old things, or find out roughly how old they are. How many years/months/weeks old are they?

Information and Communication Technology

- Use a word processor to make an inventory of all the old things in your display – sort into alphabetical order.

- Explore different fonts on a word processor to produce some old-style lettering and use these to enhance your exhibits (see photograph, above).

- Send an e-mail to your local history resource centre or museum requesting information to help plan a visit.

Humanities

- Visit a local museum. Ask the children to look closely at how the artefacts are arranged and labelled. Use the information to set up a class museum of your own. How will you classify the artefacts in your display collection: as 'Home', 'Work', 'Toys'?

- Take the children out into your locality to look for historical evidence of 'old things'. Can they spot dates on signs, buildings or monuments? What other clues can they glean from street furniture, post boxes, drain covers, lamp posts or street names?

- Ask the children about people older than themselves. Try making some generation diagrams or timelines of their own family and friends (see illustration, right).

- Compare old and new versions of similar objects, for example a hot water bottle. Consider the similarities and differences in materials, style and shape.

Art and Design

- Make close observational drawings of items from your old things collection using pencil or charcoal. Involve the children in the mounting and display of their own work. How can they complement the old things theme in their choice of mounting and display? Try silhouette mounting, browning the paper or adding a Plasticine seal.

- Try making rag rug squares using hessian, or stitch a Victorian sampler of your name.

- Look at pictures by the old masters such Constable, Turner, Leonardo da Vinci. Try working in the same style to produce a landscape painting of your locality or a still-life portrait using a collection of artefacts from your display.

Shiny Things

Getting Started

Brainstorm all the shiny things the children can think of that are found in the home and the wider environment: tin foil, Cellophane, jewellery, lights, the sun. Are they wearing anything that is shiny, such as hair slides, buckles or buttons? What shiny things can they spot around the classroom? Ask the children to collect shiny materials and objects to use for art activities, and to make a shiny stimulus display.

English

- Read *The Rainbow Fish* by Marcus Pfister (North-South Books) with the children. Discuss the shiny cover and illustrations. What was special about the shiny scales? What sort of character was the rainbow fish?

- Explore the 'sh' phoneme. Make a class list of words beginning with 'sh' (ship, shell, shirt, shoes, shark ...). Write the word 'shiny' in front of the nouns and display these pairs of words on shiny paper, shaped to enhance the alliteration, for example a shiny shark or a shiny shoe shape.

- Do some shiny handwriting. Use silver and gold crayons, felt-tip pens or glue and glitter to write words, labels or sentences about items in your collection.

- Write a story set on planet Shine. Include some descriptions of shiny trees, plants, vehicles, people and so on.

Mathematics

- Make a shiny number line: try using glue and coloured sequins, metallic paper and glitter to create 3D numerals (see photograph on page 2).

- Measure the capacity of shiny containers from the display collection, for example aluminium take-away food trays or cake trays. Find out which holds the most by filling them with rice, water or sand. Which containers hold more or less than 1 litre or measure to the nearest 100 millilitres?

- Use mirrors to draw the reflections of simple 2D shapes in a mirror line along one edge.

- Use shiny coins to practise number and money work. Can the children recognise coin values and give totals of three different coins? Help them to exchange coins for others of an equivalent value.

Information and Communication Technology

- Set up a planet Shine obstacle course and transform the roamer into a space buggy to be navigated around the obstacles.

- Use a thesaurus or dictionary facility on a word processing package to find some shiny synonyms such as bright, polished, glossy. Print them out, and add them to your shiny word bank.

- Set up a simple database of the properties of materials in your shiny display collection.

Science

- Ask the children to name the shiny materials in the classroom collection, for example metal, rock, fabric, paper, plastic and so on, and choose appropriate words to describe their properties, for example hard, soft, bendy. Record by writing descriptions around a picture of the object.

- Ask the children to suggest which items in the collection may be magnetic and how they can test their ideas. Group objects by magnetic or non-magnetic behaviour. What can the children tell you about magnetic behaviour?

- Investigate and record how you can make dull items, such as coins, brass ornaments and keys, look more shiny. Try putting them in natural light, shining torches onto them, polishing them or using reflections.

- What do the children think will happen to shiny things if they are left in water? What happens when they dry? Chart the changes that happen over two days, one week and then two weeks. Have they gone rusty?

Art and Design

- Make a shiny cover or wall display for a favourite story or information book. Try using decorated tin foil, shapes cut from Cellophane or coloured sequins (see photograph on page 30).

- Make a collage using only 'shiny materials' (see display photograph, above).

- Show the children paintings where the artist has used reflections, for example Salvador Dali, Monet, the Renaissance artists. If possible, take the children out to look at reflections of trees and clouds in rivers or ponds and paint pictures of their own.

Fabrics

Getting Started

Collect a few examples of different types of fabric such as cotton, nylon, hessian, wool, silk and patchwork. Try to include some materials with a strong multicultural feel (a sari, mirror work, perhaps an embroidered skull-cap). Who is wearing any clothes made from similar fabrics? Discuss which fabrics are patterned and which are plain. Where else have the children seen similar sorts of fabrics? Ask the children to bring in fabric samples from home to add to your collection.

English

- Share some story books with a strong fabric or pattern feel such as *Elmer* by David McKee (Red Fox), *The Patchwork Quilt* by Valerie Flournoy (Puffin Picture Books), or books with strong multi-media or collage type illustrations such as *The Very Hungry Caterpillar* by Eric Carle (Puffin Books). The children could try writing similar stories of their own, or add other characters with names such as Conrad Cotton or Silky Sam.

- What adjectives can the children think of to describe some of the fabrics, or patterns on the fabrics from the collection? Make a class list of these words. You could focus on initial consonant blends, for example bl(ack) bl(ue) or cr(eases) cr(inkles). Use the word list to build into a class fabric poem (see display photograph, above).

- Write a newspaper advertisement for a fabric shop's closing-down sale.

Mathematics

- Investigate the different standard and non-standard units that can be used for measuring a length of fabric. Practise using a metre rule or tape to measure fabric accurately. Role-play shopkeeper and customer to practise asking for and measuring specific amounts of fabric.

- Make up prices, per metre, for some of your fabrics and use them for creating number problems, for example how much would it cost to buy 2.5 metres, or enough to make a pair of trousers? Find the total cost if everyone in the class bought 1 metre.

Information and Communication Technology

- Write class, group or individual poems using a word processing package. Develop mouse control by highlighting parts of the text to change font sizes and styles to reflect the various textures of the fabrics.

- Make care labels, including the symbols, for some of your special fabrics. Look at the care labels on clothes, focusing particularly on the symbols. Use a drawing or clip art software option to design and draw them on screen.

Science

- Put swatches of fabric in a feely bag. Can the children identify which fabric is which by touch alone?

- Take out threads from different fabrics such as rope, hessian or wool. Look at them under a magnifier, and make careful observational drawings. Label them.

- How durable are different fabrics? Try rubbing hard, uneven objects such as wood or stones over pieces of cotton, silk, wool, polyester and denim. Which fabrics take the longest to tear, wear or fray? What conclusions can the children draw about different fabrics and their possible uses?

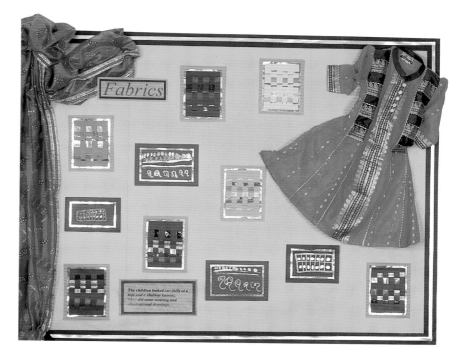

- Predict, test and chart what happens to different fabrics when you put them in water. Which leak colour? Which dry the quickest? Do any of them shrink? Try the test first with cold and then hot water.

- Ask the children to conduct a survey around the school of fabrics that have been used for particular purposes, for example curtains, cushions and chair covers. What reasons can they deduce about why particular fabrics have been used?

Art and Design

- Use brightly coloured fabrics, such as saris, as the stimulus for some shiny weaving patterns (see display photograph, left).

- Look at traditional and decorative designs used on fabrics in African, Asian or Muslim countries. Try some designs of your own in a similar style. For example, you could make rangoli or mendhi patterns from chalk or coloured seeds.

- Give the children a small piece of fabric to incorporate into a bigger painting or pastel picture. For example, a swirly blue pattern could become part of the sea, or some orange printed circles could represent the sun.

- Make a textured, feely greetings card for a special friend, or elderly relative.

Things for Making a Mark

Getting Started

Collect some everyday mark-makers from around the classroom: pencils, felt-tip pens, crayons, chalk and paint brushes. Can the children work out what these things have in common? What other things can they think of that are used for making marks? The list might include computer programs, hands, charcoal, and patterning tools for pottery.

English

- Set up a special writing corner for young writers to practise their handwriting. Provide a range of writing tools and other mark-makers from your collection, and a variety of paper in different shapes, sizes and colours. Make sure all the children use the writing corner regularly for short, guided activities.

- Give groups of children different mark-makers to practise writing and recognising the letter strings in their names. Group these according to initial letter sounds or common letter strings.

- Give the children different mark-makers to practise writing. Ask them to write a sentence for each implement, stating its best use. For example, in crayon the children could write: 'Crayons are for colouring pictures.'

- Using a range of different writing tools, make a variety of marks, such as wavy lines, zig-zags and spirals, on a flip chart. Can the children think of adjectives to describe the different marks (thin, spidery, blotchy, smooth).

Mathematics

- Make sequences with different mark-makers, for example short/long/short crayons. Can a friend continue and describe the sequence? Develop the use of ordinal numbers by asking questions such as, 'What position is the fourth red crayon in?' or 'What colour would the nineteenth crayon be in this pattern of crayons?'

- Find ways of sorting your mark-makers into sets, for example those with/without lids, those that make coloured/black marks or thick/thin marks.

- Draw a variety of straight lines using different markers. Estimate, then measure the length of each line using standard or non-standard units of measurement. Make a wavy line on a piece of paper and ask the children how it can be measured.

Information and Communication Technology

- Take the mouse for a mark-making walk around the screen. Try adding different colours to make interesting patterns, or pathways and mazes to print out. Other children can then follow them with a pencil.

- Develop mouse control by asking the children to practise writing their name on screen using a painting or drawing program. Explore different colours and thicknesses of line. Print out the names (see photograph, left).

Science

- Which mark-makers are waterproof? Try dripping a few drops of water on to patterns made by different markers – felt-tip pens, ink, chalk, pastels and permanent markers. Which patterns run? Record your observations.

- Which marks fade quickest? Observe and record what happens to blocks of colour made by different mark-markers when they are left in sunlight for a certain length of time.

- Help the children to set up chromatography tests to see how the pigments in ink can be separated. The simplest way is to make a mark with a felt-tip or ink pen in the middle of a circle of filter paper, drip some water on to the mark and observe how the colours separate out in circles. Experiment with different colours and record the results.

Art and Design

- Use a range of mark-markers such as hard/soft pencils, wax/lead crayons or pastels to make rubbings of tree bark, stones, bricks or coins. Which mark-markers do the children think produce the best rubbings? They could go on to use their rubbings to make pictures such as woodland scenes or buildings.

- Explore mark-making on fabric. Use a needle and coloured threads to sew patterns on a square piece of felt. Try to create zig-zag lines, wavy lines and thick and thin stitches.

- Experiment with mark-making in malleable materials such as dough or clay. Scratch, press or indent a pattern with some of your mark-makers into a clay tile. Make a decorated clay pot to store pencils or paint brushes.

- Encourage the children to explore different mark-making effects by painting patterns with brushes of various widths, and by using the brushes in different ways, for example spatter prints, pointillism effects.

- Look at the work of artists like Jackson Pollock. Encourage the children to pour, drip, squirt and spray paints to create a variety of spontaneous designs.

Round Things

Getting Started

Asking the children to name all the round things they can think of will result in more items than your display table could hold! You could narrow your brainstorm down by restricting it to different themes, for example round things on our clothes, round toys and games, round things in the class-room, natural round things. Discuss the difference between a flat, 2D round shape and a 3D round shape, or sphere.

English

- Share with the children the book, *The Village of Round and Square Houses* by Ann Grifalconi (Macmillan). Try adding an alternative ending or retelling the story from the point of view of a different character.

- Make up circle stories using one or two of your round items as prompts, for example a red balloon or a button. You could scribe the story on a flip chart as you go along and write up the final draft as a round book.

- Teach the song, 'The Wheels on the Bus go Round and Round' and enjoy making your own version of each verse. Add accompaniment to the song using round instruments such as tambourines, drums and shakers. Other songs with a round theme include, 'Here We Go Round the Mulberry Bush' or 'Ring O' Roses'.

- Provide the children with a variety of pens, pencils and crayons to practise writing letters which are formed with rounded movements of the hand: o, q, c, b, d and p. Mount them on round paper to add to your display.

Mathematics

- Use hoops or old bicycle tyres to show sets of round things.

- Practise rounding numbers to the nearest 10, 20 and 100.

- Do some clock mathematics. Practise saying the numbers round the clock face, establishing how the hands move round. Practise counting in 5s. Read the time and work out how many minutes past the hour it is, counting in 5s. How many hours and minutes until lunch or home time?

- Ask the children to draw round a circle and describe its properties in terms of corners and sides and whether they are curved or straight. Also look for circular faces on a variety of 3D shapes and everyday objects.

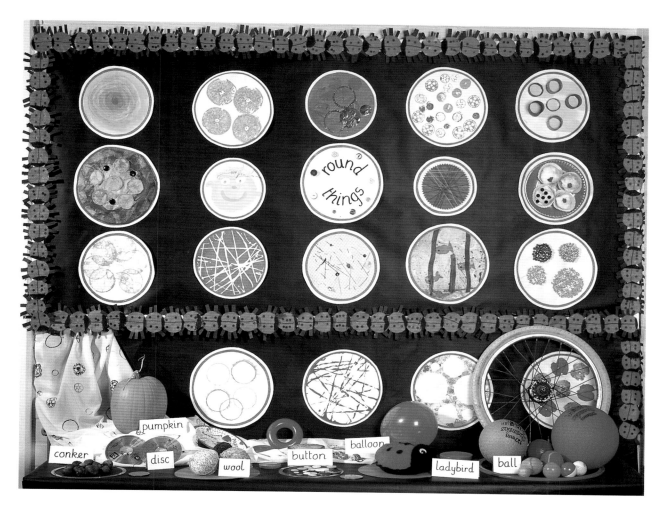

Information and Communication Technology

- Use a computer drawing package to draw circles on screen. Interlock circles of different sizes and use the paint facility to change the colours of the interlocking sectors to create interesting patterns and designs.

- Programme the roamer to travel and turn through different degrees of a circle. How can you make the roamer turn a full circle, make a half turn or quarter turn?

Science

- Investigate which balls bounce best. Try tennis balls, footballs, balls of wool and rubber balls. Encourage the children to predict first and then test. Were there any surprises? Show the results in a simple picture chart.

- Set up some ramps of different angled inclines for a marble to roll down. Compare and record how long it takes the marbles to reach the end.

Art and Design

- Make a close observational drawing of a wheel, or other selected item from your round things collection.

- Let the children enjoy printing with a variety of round items (for example cogs, rolled marbles, pieces of fruit) on round paper, create a collage or sew pictures of circular items such as pizzas, port holes and cakes (see display photograph, above).

- Design and make a round greetings card using round patterns for decoration.

- Use circles of tissue paper or pre-cut sticky circles to create overlapping circular patterns and designs.

- Blow some bubbles with the children and talk about their round, spherical shape and the colours they can see as the light shines through. Try making bubble prints by blowing through a straw to create a bubbly effect.

Red Things

Getting Started

You could begin by playing some I-spy type games: Who's wearing something red today? How many red objects can the children see around the room? What other things can they think of that are red? Think of something red, ask the children to guess what you may be thinking of by asking questions to which you may only answer yes or no, for example 'Is it a fruit?' 'Do you wear it?' Build your red collection with the children over a day or two, encouraging them to bring in interesting red things from home.

English

- Share stories with a red theme, for example *Little Red Riding Hood*, or *Little Red Train to the Rescue* by Benedict Blathwayt (Red Fox) and *Red is Best* by Kathy Stinson (Oxford University Press). Try making up your own versions of the stories, or adding more red descriptions and adjectives to the original.

- Make a picture/word list of all the red things in your collection. Identify those with the consonant-vowel-consonant spelling pattern, for example bag, hat, bat. How many of your collection objects are plurals (marbles, balls, gloves and so on)?

- Compose a red class poem. What words can the children think of that rhyme with red? Try adding a recurring rhythm (see display photograph on page 39).

Mathematics

- Place a variety of beads, counters or construction kit pieces in a bag. Ask the children to grab a handful and count how many red items they are holding. Record the number and repeat.

- Use beads, bricks, or construction kit pieces to continue a sequence, for example red, yellow, red. Try other sequences: red, red, yellow, red, red. Older or more able children could try recording their sequences on squared paper.

- Sort the red objects in the display into different shapes, for example round, square, hexagonal red things or 2D and 3D red things. Describe mathematical properties and positions such as shape, size, curves, number of straight edges and corners.

- Survey favourite class colours. How many children like red best? Represent the results as a 3D graph using coloured interlocking cubes.

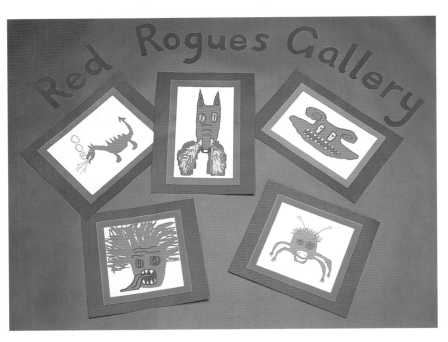

Information and Communication Technology

- Practise spelling the word 'red' by using a keyboard. Try using different font sizes, styles and shades of colour.

- Use a paint or draw computer program to create red pictures. These could be red monsters or fantastical creatures. Print them out to make a Red Rogues Gallery. If you do not have a colour printer you could print out the designs and then use a range of media to colour and decorate them (see photograph, left).

Science

- Make an illustrated list with the children of the sorts of places where red is used in the environment as a safety or warning colour (for example traffic lights, hazard warning triangles and road signs). Take the children on a 'red walk' to look at the use of red in the environment.

- Investigate further why red is used to warn us of danger. Which colours can you see from furthest away? Test primary colours (red, blue, yellow) and dark and light colours. Chart the results.

- Does red fade more quickly than other colours when exposed to sunlight? Leave pieces of red, blue, green or other coloured fabrics or tissue paper on a window sill for a week. Observe and record what happens to the colours.

Art and Design

- Practise colour mixing. Add varying amounts of white paint to a basic red to make lighter tones. Use these new shades of red to reinforce shapes (large and small circles, rectangles, hexagons) and to practise brush control (see display photograph, above).

- Mix warm, red colours and other shades of the primary colours blue and yellow. Tear, scrunch and cut your results to make a fiery collage against a dark blue sky.

- Try using red fruits and vegetables, such as raspberries, redcurrants and beetroot, to dye some plain fabric. How many different shades of red can you produce?

- Design and make a Little Red Riding Hood cape to fit a soft toy.

Lights

Getting Started

Brainstorm all the different kinds of lights the children know about: electric lights, fluorescent strip lighting, lamps, bicycle lights, candles, torches, traffic lights and so on. Ask them to bring in some examples to display. Talk about the importance of light in celebrations such as Diwali, Hanukkah, Holi and Christmas.

English

- Read the children stories which strongly feature light, such as *The Owl Who was Afraid of the Dark* by Jill Tomlinson (Mammoth), or *Can't You Sleep, Little Bear?* by Martin Waddell (Walker Books). How did light help the characters feel less afraid at night? Discuss and write about how the children feel about night-time.

- Which words rhyme with 'light'? Can the children spell them out by analogy? For example bright, fright, night, right and sight. You could display the 'ight' words on a candle or light bulb outline, or put them into a book in the shape of a bulb or candle.

- Give the children a selection of lights. Why do we have these? What would life be like without them? You could display your information as a 'Lights Fact File'.

- Write a safety leaflet for the safe use of candles, including rules such as 'Always use a candle-holder' and 'Never walk around with a lighted candle'.

Mathematics

- Make a simple picture sequence of what children do during daylight hours, for example between 8 am and 5 pm, either during the week or at weekends.

- Collect data to find out who has a bedside lamp (or who goes to bed with a night-light on). Present the results as a tally chart or pictogram.

- Investigate how many days, weeks, months it is until Diwali, Hanukkah, Christmas or another festival. Make a candle-shaped count down chart or calendar to keep track of the days.

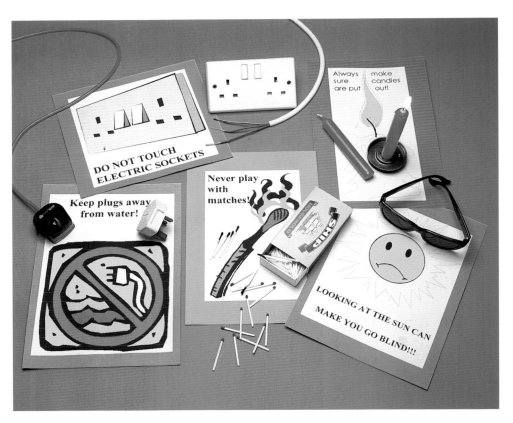

Information and Communication Technology

- Enter information about lights on to a database. Discuss the fields you will use, such as the name of the light (for example torch, oil lamp); power source (electricity, oil); where you might use it (attic, kitchen); and its purpose.

- Use a paint or art program to design and draw safety symbols to help others identify the potential dangers of lights, power points and naked flames (see photograph, left).

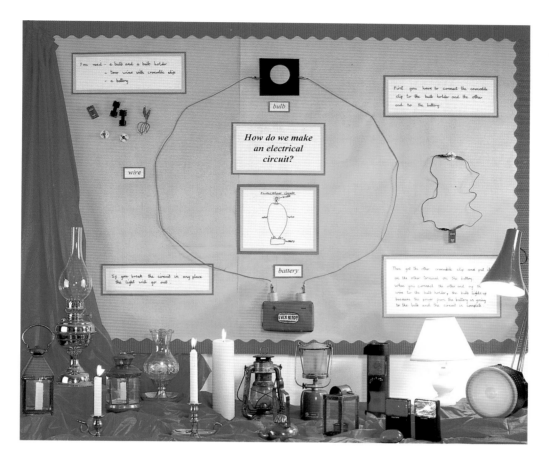

Science

- Make a chart to show how the lights in your collection can be classified, for example according to how they are powered (batteries, electricity, oil and wax).

- Investigate the links between lights and safety. Look at lights on the road (traffic lights, pedestrian crossing symbols), light reflectors on bicycles and reflective strips on bags and clothes. Ask the children how they can make themselves more visible at night. Compare and test the reflective strips on children's bags and coats. What is needed to make them shine or show up?

- Give the children a collection of batteries, insulated wires, bulbs and buzzers. Help them to set up electrical circuits. Can they write or draw some step by step instructions for others to follow? (See the display photograph, above.) Reinforce the learning by giving some children examples of circuits that do not work, and challenging them to make the bulb light up. Can they explain how they made it work?

Humanities

- Research the importance of candles and lights in celebrations such as Diwali or Hanukkah. Invite a parent or community member into school to talk to the children about their special celebration. You could try making diwas (the small oil lamps Hindus light during Diwali).

- Find out how people's homes were lit before electricity was used. Present your findings as a simple 'Lighting Then and Now' display.

Art and Design

- Use drawing pencils to make still-life drawings of lights in your display collection. Focus particularly on light and shade, and encourage the children to explore different pencil techniques to achieve varying depths of light and shadow.

- Explore how we can make lighter tones by colour mixing. Explore the effects of adding different amounts of white paint to a particular colour, for example red or blue, and make patterns with the new colour range.

- Design and make a candle-holder from clay or Plasticine.

Measuring Devices

Getting Started

Set up a simple stimulus collection of measuring devices from the resources and equipment you already have in and around school. Brainstorm with the children all the things we use for measuring: rulers, tapes, scales, balances, growth charts, measuring jugs, clocks and stop watches – the list is almost endless. Encourage the class to add to the starter display by bringing measuring devices in from home.

English

- Read with the children books about size and growth: *Titch* by Pat Hutchins (Red Fox), *Flat Stanley* by Jeff Brown (Mammoth), *Jim and the Beanstalk* by Raymond Briggs (Puffin) and *The Shrinking of Treehorn* by Florence Parry Heide (Puffin). Consider how the authors describe the changing size of the main characters. What kinds of measures were used? How did the characters feel?

- Compile a simple information book about measuring devices. Draw the items and write a caption for each one. Think of a good title. The book could be divided into sections, perhaps devices for measuring length, time, volume or weight.

- Develop the vocabulary of measurement by asking the children to brainstorm words associated with time, for example minute, hour, second, earlier, later, before, after, half, quarter, past and to. Repeat for length, weight, capacity and so on. Display the vocabulary alongside the appropriate measuring devices.

Mathematics

- Practise counting using the number lines on rulers, tapes and other suitable measuring devices. Count forwards and backwards in 1s, 2s, 5s and 10s.

- Set the children some timed challenges using a variety of different timers. For example, how many times can you hop or say the 5 times table before the sand-timer runs out? Count and chart how many 10-high interlocking cube towers you can build in one minute using a stop clock.

- Collect five items of a similar size from around the classroom. Estimate then weigh each item using standard or non-standard measures. Record the objects in order of weight.

- Use a tape measure to measure and label the shortest and longest shelf or bookcase in the classroom. How many of these shelves could you fit along your longest or shortest wall?

- Use measuring jugs and beakers to practise estimating, measuring and recording capacity. Set capacity problems such as: If this jug holds 500 millilitres of orange juice, how much would 3 jugs hold?

Information and Communication Technology

- Record how many different sorts of digital measuring devices the children use in classroom activities. Help them to read digital scales, numbers on video players, tape recorders and timers, and to use calculators to reinforce number work.

Art and Design

- Stitch a clock point design. Punch 12 holes in a card to represent the numbers on a clockface. Take the thread from hole number 1 (1 o'clock) to hole number 7 (7 o'clock) then round the back of the card to number 2, back to number 8 and so on all the way round the clock (see photograph, above).

- Make close observational drawings of some of your measuring devices, for example watches, clocks and cogs.

- Design, make and decorate a growth chart for the classroom or school hall. Ask children to measure and chart their growth rate over a term.

- Make rocking animal pendulums (see illustration, left). These work on the same principle as the commercially-produced, rocking timers. Fold a paper plate in half to make the rocking mechanism. For the front, let the children choose an animal design and decorate it with felt-tip pens. Attach features such as a head, tails or ears, to the paper plate. When complete use the animal pendulum to reinforce number and time work: how many times does the dog rock in one minute?

43

Comics, Catalogues and Magazines

Getting Started

Ask the children to collect their favourite comics, magazines and any unwanted catalogues from home. Try to include some magazines on special interests, such as cycling, riding or handicrafts. Ask the children what they enjoy about comics and magazines. Look carefully at the different formats and styles and discuss the proportion of text to pictures. Read some books that have a comic strip format (graphic novels) such as Asterix books, *The Snowman* by Raymond Briggs (Puffin) and *Dear Daddy* by Philippe Dupasquier (Picture Puffin).

English

- Look at comics and books with minimal or no text, such as *Dear Daddy* by Philippe Dupasquier, and ask the children to act out, tell or write the story.

- Look at how speech is shown in comics, magazines and some graphic novels. Ask the children to make a three-frame cartoon or picture and caption sequence of the funniest thing they can remember happening to them or a friend or relative.

- Make an alphabetical reference list of the subject areas represented by your collection of magazines and catalogues; for example, cooking, DIY, fishing, mountain bikes.

- Create your own class comic or magazine. Think of an appropriate name for it and discuss what you would like to include in the contents; for example, interviews, features of general interest, puzzles, competitions and advertisements.

Mathematics

- Use pictures from catalogues to make a matching sets game (see photograph, right). Children take turns to pick up the cards and place them in the correct set on the baseboard. Extend the game by asking the children to make more sets and pictures of their own.

- Survey favourite comics, magazines or comic-strip characters. Show the data as a pictogram. Ask the children to make statements about the data and display these alongside the pictogram.

- Select pages from a catalogue for the children to look at. Make sure the pages show the prices of the items. Pose some number challenges such as: How much is the cheapest/most expensive item on the page? If you paid a set amount per month, how long would it take to pay for the most expensive item?

- Investigate the cost of a particular weekly magazine. How much would you spend if you bought one every week for a month, six months or one year?

Information and Communication Technology

- Use a computer drawing package to draw some favourite comic characters on screen. Print out three different characters to make a new cartoon family and tell or write stories about their escapades.

- Ask the children to think of captions to accompany your collection of comics, magazines and catalogues, and write them on screen using a word processor. Encourage the children to draft and redraft their caption using the delete and cut-and-paste facilities.

Humanities

- Look at and discuss comic characters from different times and historical periods, for example Asterix.

- Create your own comic cartoon characters to reflect the particular period of history you may be studying. These might include Roman and Viking warriors, Greek gods or Egyptian mummies.

Art and Design

- Cut out magazine and catalogue pictures and use them to create collage landscapes as settings for cartoon characters. You could create camouflage backgrounds (see photograph, right).

- Design a front cover for a new children's magazine.

- Design and make a simple magazine rack. Consider with the children what it could be made from, perhaps thick cardboard, wood or an empty carton. You could add partitions to separate different comics or magazines.

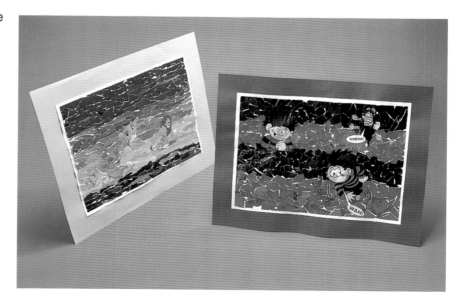

Things That Make Us Laugh

Getting Started

Tell the children a joke, or share a funny, personal story. What other sorts of things make the children laugh – cartoons, jokes, clowns, comic characters, TV personalities or the antics and sense of humour of other members of the family?

English

- Share some funny books with the children (see Very Funny Books, page 50). Can the children recount three things in a story that made them laugh out loud? The children could act out one of the stories.

- Use a puppet or clown to tell a funny story. Talk to the children about how they can use their voice as well as physical actions to add to the humour.

- Make a picture or word list of items you might find in a clown's prop or costume bag.

- Make up a cartoon sequence showing a real-life event that made you laugh, or literally illustrate something that 'tickled you pink'.

- Compile a class book of favourite jokes (see photograph, above). Can the children think of a good title for their class book? What shape could they make the book, perhaps a smiling face or exclamation mark? Have a joke-telling session at the end of the week where children can choose and read their favourite joke from the book.

- Create a new cartoon character that makes you laugh. Draw the character and then add descriptive labels to show, for example, the character's name, and funny features such as sticky yellow hair, or silly glasses and clothes. Put some of these characters together and invent stories to tell the rest of the class.

- How many words can you find to describe laughter? The list might include giggle, chuckle, grin, howl. Sometimes we make up words to match the sound of laughter such as 'ha ha ha'. Can you find other ways of representing the sounds of laughter? How might we spell them?

Mathematics

- How many different funny faces can the children make using 4 semicircles, 2 triangles and 3 circles? Try varying the number of shapes and rotating them to get different expressions.

- Make sequences by drawing laughing or sad faces. For example, a sequence might show one laughing face and then one sad face, or two sad faces followed by one laughing face, and so on.

- Conduct a survey of favourite comedy programmes or cartoon characters. Present the data as a pictogram of laughing faces.

- Look at the running times of cartoon videos and record which are the shortest and longest. How long would it take to watch three of them?

Information and Communication Technology

- Use a drawing or painting program to make clown pictures or smiling faces. Print them out, add a speech bubble and write a joke inside the bubble.

- Record favourite jokes or read extracts from humorous novels on to a tape recorder to cheer somebody up who is not feeling very well. You could send a fax or e-mail to the manager of your local hospital radio asking if they would like a sample of the tape.

- Take some photographs of your friends laughing and make a montage for your classroom door. You could try making a video of some comic sketches devised by the children for a younger class to enjoy during wet playtimes.

Art and Design

- Which colours do the children associate with laughing or being happy? Explore the effects of colour and mood by painting the same picture but in happy and sad colours.

- Make a funny pop-up card (or card with a funny face or joke) to cheer somebody up who is not feeling very well.

- Make clown puppets or use face paints to create a funny clown face on a friend. Finish by adding a red nose.

- Get animated! Try designing and making spinning cards, based on a favourite cartoon character or creature (see diagram, right).

Spinning card

Soft Toys

Getting Started

You may want to begin by bringing a soft toy of your own into the classroom and talking to the children about its history – why you still have it, or to whom it belongs, its name and a memorable event in which it was involved. Encourage the children to recount stories about a favourite soft toy of their own. Invite them to bring in a soft toy for a short time, to build up a display.

English

- Enjoy sharing stories about soft toys. Try *Old Bear* or *Little Bear's Trousers* by Jane Hissey (Red Fox), or *Jamaica's Find* by Juanita Havill and Anne Sibley O'Brien (Mammoth). What other stories do the children know about soft toys? Can they retell one in their own words?

- Ask the children to introduce their soft toy to the rest of the class. They should say at least one sentence about it, for example 'This is Frozo the frog.' or 'I like to cuddle my teddy bear George when I feel sad.' Help the class to devise a series of questions to ask the owner to find out more about the soft toy: 'How did you get your soft toy?' 'What games do you play with it?' 'Where does your soft toy live?'

- Write a short sentence about why your soft toy is so special. Add these descriptions to your display (see display photograph on page 49).

- Make an initial sound soft toy shop. Ask the children to label the toys with the correct initial sound cards, for example 't' for teddy, 'p' for penguin, and then put them in alphabetical order on the shelves. Play games asking the children to identify all the toys beginning with a particular letter.

Mathematics

- Sort soft toys into sets, for example according to colour of fur or hair, size of toy or type of animal. Use hoops to show the sets.

- Measure some of the soft toys using standard and non-standard units. For example, how many interlocking cubes or centimetres high are the tallest and shortest? You could measure the fattest and thinnest with a length of string.

- Play some soft toy mental number games. For example, estimate how many soft toys are in the display altogether, then count and check the results. Whose guess was closest? Put the toys in pairs and count in twos. How many soft toys would there be if 2, 4 or 6 children took their toys home?

Information and Communication Technology

- The children may enjoy taking photographs of their favourite soft toys, or taking a picture of a friend with his or her teddy. You could make these into a class album.

- Import pictures of soft toys (many software packages have pictures of pandas, teddy bears, etc.). Print out, and add a name for them. You could use these for seasonal cards (see photograph, left), or go on to use them as a starting point for storyboard activities.

Humanities

- Find out more about some of the real animals represented in your soft toy display, such as bears, pandas, hippos and tigers. Compile a class book showing the soft toy on one side of the double-page spread, and a picture of the real animal drawn or cut out of a magazine on the other. Write simple captions under each picture, for example 'This is my teddy bear Alfonso. This is a real bear from Canada.'

- Can the children recall or research well-known stories about bears, for example *Goldilocks and the Three Bears*, *Winnie the Pooh* or *Paddington Bear*? They could try retelling or acting out parts of these stories.

Art and Design

- Make soft toy blob prints by using thick paint to create a soft toy painting on one side of a folded sheet of paper. Fold it over carefully while still wet to make an identical print on the second side. Use these prints to enhance your display.

- Provide a variety of containers, for example cardboard or plastic boxes, paper, string and plastic bags or sheets of wrapping paper to make a container to keep a soft toy safe and clean when moving house.

- Make finger puppets of your favourite soft toys.

- Plan a teddy bear's picnic. What might be a teddy's favourite food and drink, for example honey sandwiches for Pooh bear? The children could make sandwiches, decorate the plates and design the invitations.

Very Funny Books

Getting Started

Revisit some humorous picture books, short novels and poetry that you have enjoyed reading with the children. Which ones do they like best – why? Encourage the children to recall the names of some of the characters from favourite funny books and recount actions and storylines. Ask the children to bring in a favourite funny book from home to add to your starter collection.

English

- Encourage the children to take turns reading, or acting out extracts from some of their favourite funny stories for the rest of the class. Ask them to practise using different voices and techniques to emphasise the humour.

- Think about the characters in some of the children's favourite funny books and talk about why they make us laugh so much. Do the children know any similar, real-life characters?

- You could make the sharing of very funny books a literacy theme for a day or two, and invite family members in to school to enjoy them with you. This is also a good opportunity to share humorous stories from a range of countries and cultures.

- Look more closely at the books in your collection and consider how we know that they are going to be funny. What clues can we pick up from the cover?

- Compile a big book of reviews to recommend funny books for others to read (see photograph on page 51).

- Make up a funny class poem with the children about laughter or a humorous literary character. Use a simple rhythm and rhyming pattern to complement the light tone.

- Choose a favourite funny picture book and try writing a new story in a similar style.

Mathematics

- Count the pages in your favourite funny book. How many would there be if you added 2, 4, 5 or 10 more? How many would there be if the author had written 3 or 4 pages less? How many if there were only half as many?

- Sort your class collection of funny books into further sets, for example those by the same author/illustrator.

- Estimate the number of words on a page of one of your funny books. Help the children to work out strategies for counting them, for example count the number of words on a line, then the number of lines and multiply the two numbers.

- Investigate and measure the dimensions of some of your funny books using standard or non-standard measures. Look at the differences in shape. Which are square/rectangular? Which one has the largest area? Use squared paper to find out.

Information and Communication Technology

- Many publishers have their own Web sites. Help the children to find the publishers of their favourite funny book on the Internet.

- Send an e-mail or fax to the publisher or author of your favourite funny book with your views and comments. Try sending it in rhyming verse.

- Set up a computer database for the children to keep a log of the funny books they bring into school. This can be printed out and then filled in by hand, or saved as a file on the computer to be accessed and updated by the children.

Art and Design

- Design and make alternative covers for some of the funny books in your collection. What are the best colours and media to use? You could try making a collage or 3D version.

- Make models or masks of favourite funny book characters, for example the monster in *Not Now, Bernard* by David McKee (Red Fox) or the aliens from *Here Come the Aliens by* Colin McNaughton *(Walker Books).* Discuss the most appropriate materials to use, for example discarded packaging, shredded paper or Plasticine/playdough.

- Look at the art techniques used by the illustrators in some of your funny books, for example spatter printing with bright colours on black paper in *Here Come the Aliens*, black and white ink cartoons in *Bill's New Frock* by Anne Fine (Mammoth), pastel work in *The Story of the Little Mole Who Knew it was None of His Business* by Werner Holzwarth (David Bennett Books), and the mixed-media feel of David McKee's *Not Now, Bernard*. Try out some of these techniques and use them to illustrate your own stories and books.

Sporty Things

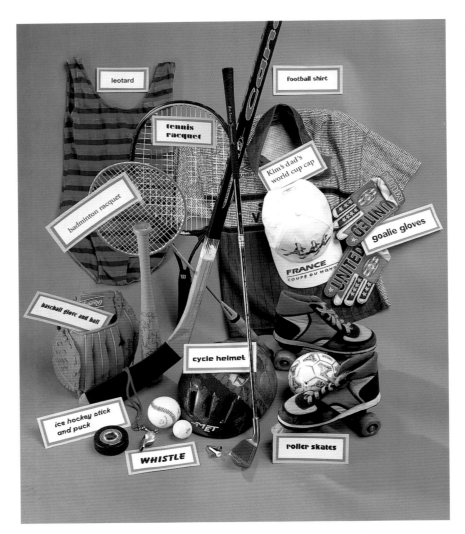

labels in image: leotard · football shirt · tennis racquet · Kim's dad's world cup cap · badminton racquet · goalie gloves · baseball glove and ball · cycle helmet · ice hockey stick and puck · WHISTLE · roller skates

Getting Started

A good way to introduce this topic is to provide a small stimulus collection of items related to sport. Can the children work out what the items have in common? (The age of the children will dictate how obvious or subtle you make the items.) Talk about favourite sports, the sorts of clothes worn and the equipment used. Ask the children to bring in a sporty item to display.

English

- Brainstorm as many sports as possible. Circle one of the compound words in your class list, for example 'football' and explain that it is a word made up of two words. Ask the children to identify and find other sporty compound words to record and illustrate.

- Describe the rules of a particular sport or game to someone who has never played it before. What happens when a player breaks the rules? Use the information to compile an illustrated rule book for your particular sport.

- Show in three- or four-captioned frames a sporting sequence, for example diving into a swimming pool, swimming a length and climbing out the other end, or kicking a ball, a goalkeeper diving, a ball in the net.

- Explore active verbs such as run, jump and swim – what is their function in sentences? Ask the children to identify the past and present tense for each active verb: for example, run = ran, running.

- Talk about the sorts of feelings the children have when playing sports. Do they feel excited and nervous before an important match? You could ask them to consider what it might feel like actually to be a particular sporty item, for example a pair of roller blades or a football. Use your discussions as a stimulus for writing poetry.

Mathematics

- Use TV guides and newspapers to monitor and record, in chart and graph form, how much time is given to sports programmes on television and radio over a week. On which days are there most/least sports? What type of sport gets the most coverage? What are the most popular times for showing sports programmes?

- How many different team strips can the children make by using combinations of, for example, red, yellow and blue, for shirts, shorts and socks?

- Set sporty number challenges for the children to work out in their heads, for example if a player scored two goals in three matches and one goal in another, how many did he or she score altogether?

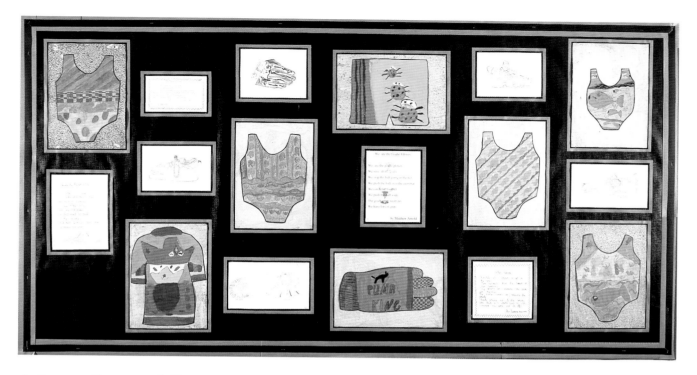

Information and Communication Technology

- Use a word processor to write labels for items in your sporty things display. Practise using different font styles and sizes.

- Design class sports certificates for rewarding good sporting behaviour.

- Video a class team game or show children a short video of a football match. Replay the excerpt and ask the children to take turns at giving a commentary.

Science

- Name and describe the materials used for making items of sports equipment from the display collection, for example wood, metal, plastic and leather. Group together and label equipment made from the same material.

- Challenge the children to find things within the sports collection that need or use either a 'push' or a 'pull' to make them move, for example ball, hockey stick, tennis racquet. Add appropriate labels to these items.

- Talk with the children about what is meant by exercise and being healthy. Identify different types of exercise children can do outside school and encourage them to notice changes that take place in their bodies as they exercise. Ask the children to create posters to promote exercise at break time. Laminate and display these in the school playground.

Art and Design

- Make close observational drawings and paintings of some of your sporty things. Display on appropriately coloured marbled backgrounds, for example blues for swimwear, greens for team field games (see photographs, above and right).

- Design logos for a new sportswear label or sports team.

- Make 'sporty things' montages from pictures cut out of magazines, newspapers and unwanted posters.

- Make a card body with moving joints attached with brass paper-fasteners. Explore the sporty movements that you can make the body perform and draw round the outline on paper. Select an athletic pose and repeat it as a shadow to give a sense of movement.

Games

Getting Started

With the whole class, play a well-known game, such as hangman, or a cumulative memory game like 'I packed my bag and in it I put ...' (for example, things beginning with the letter 'e'). Ask the children what other games they enjoy. Focus particularly on board games or table-top games such as cards and dominoes. Can the children explain the rules verbally for some of these games? Ask them to bring in a favourite game to begin the display collection.

English

- Make initial letter or consonant blend dominoes. Match 'sp' or 'ch' words with the correct pictures to make a line (see illustration, right). Adapt the idea for other phonic activities such as consonant-vowel-consonant words and pictures.

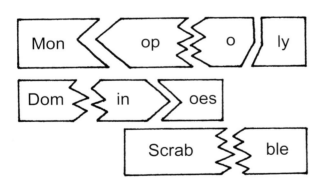

- Use the names from the favourite games collection to develop syllabification. Split up the words into syllables and clap or beat the number of syllables in each game, for example Monopoly has four syllables (see illustration, left).

- Challenge the children to make up a word search. Focus on certain letter strings or hide the names of the games from the classroom collection in the letter squares.

- Make up a new playground rhyme with a strong rhythm so that it can be used for playing skipping games.

Mathematics

- Play mathematics games with skipping ropes. Examples: How many skips can you count before the sand timer runs out? How can you make triangles, squares or circles with skipping ropes?

- Challenge the children to make up their own number problems. Write two or three simple digits on separate pieces of card, for example 1, 5, 7 or 4, 3, 6, and ask the children how many different numbers they can make. How many different multiples can they make?

- Encourage those children who have a firm grasp of number facts to 100 to make up some calculator games. For example, in 'Beat the Calculator' can one player add or subtract two numbers faster than the other player can work out the answer with a calculator?

Information and Communication Technology

- Practise mouse control or keyboard skills by playing control or simulation games on the computer, for example word and sound recognition games, number or adventure games.

- Make up a circuit game for two or more players and a roamer. This could be based on a nursery rhyme or story such as *Little Red Riding Hood* or *The Jolly Postman* by Janet and Allan Ahlberg (Heinemann Young Books). Set out items for the roamer to stop and 'collect' around the circuit, such as presents for Grandma.

Humanities

- Try to find out the history of and some interesting facts about a favourite toy or game. You could present your findings as a 'History of Games' book to keep as a classroom resource.

- Investigate playground games such as marbles or skipping. How did these games originate? Have the rules changed over time? Write and illustrate the origins of names for marbles of different values, for example Chinas, Tiger's Eye or Bloody Mary.

- Invite an older community member into school to talk to the children about the toys and games they enjoyed as a child.

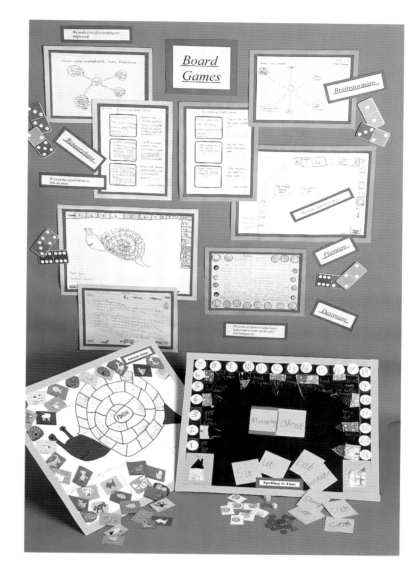

Art and Design

- Design and make a board game of your own. Encourage the children to work logically through the thinking and planning stages and record their ideas, drafts and stages of development. You could begin by asking them to use the library or the Internet to do some research. How are games classified? Make sure the children can explain the rules of the games they invent.

- Give the game a name. Can the children design a box for their board game and a leaflet to advertise it?

- Make a jigsaw puzzle from an old greetings card or calendar, mounted on stiff card.

Maps

Getting Started

Begin by creating a stimulus collection of different types of maps. Talk to the children about how they would find their way to a place if they did not know the route. Discuss the sorts of information a map gives and consider different kinds of maps and where the children may have seen them – for example on a nature trail walk, on postcards or in holiday brochures. Make sure they understand the basic idea of scale (that the map is a small, but accurate representation of a large area).

English

- Build up a word bank of 'map language', for example scale, left, right, north, south, east, west, river, road, contour and symbol. Fold and display the word bank like a map.

- Describe a route you know well, for example from the classroom to the hall, home to school or home to the cinema. Which landmarks could you include so that other people could find their way?

- Read or tell some stories which have a theme of moving from place to place, for example *Rosie's Walk* by Pat Hutchins (Picture Puffins), *The Nut Map* by Susanna Gretz (Mammoth), *The Jolly Postman* by Janet and Allan Ahlberg (Heinemann Young Books), *Little Red Riding Hood* and *Jack and the Beanstalk*. Focus the children's attention on the directional and prepositional words, for example <u>through</u> the woods, <u>over</u> the stream, <u>past</u> the post office. Draw a simple picture map based on the story's route and make labels of the prepositions to stick on the picture.

Mathematics

- Open out folded maps and count and record how many folds and sections there are. Try folding a piece of plain paper in the same way as one of your maps.

- How many different numbers can the children make from 3- and 4-digit road numbers, for example the A427 or the B4047?

- Use a large-scale local map to survey children's routes to school. Make a chart or graph to show which roads are most frequently used and who has the longest and shortest journeys. Is there one road that is used most often?

- Work out the distance between two towns or cities on a map. How long would it take to travel there at 30 mph?

Information and Communication Technology

- Build a model of a route outlined in a story such as *Rosie's Walk*, and programme a roamer to follow the route. (See photograph, right.)

- Use a logo or control package to develop control language and positional vocabulary; for example, 'forward 4' and 'right 90 degrees'.

- Let the children use a photocopier to enlarge sections of maps so that they can work more easily with them. Tasks could include locating their own house and studying road or rail networks or the course of a river.

Humanities

- Help the children to identify the location of their school or home on a map of the area. What other landmarks such as rivers or main roads can they name?

- Look at a section of a map with the children (you may want to enlarge it) and ask them how they could get from one town or city to another. Is there a railway line, or would they go by car? Which roads would they have to go on? Could they cycle?

- Look at the signs and symbols used on maps and make a big chart with pictures and captions to help the children learn them. Symbols could include those used for a church, youth hostel, railway line, bus and coach station.

- Look for natural features on maps such as rivers, hills, mountains and the sea. Look at how they are represented on maps.

- Create maps of story settings such as *Rosie's Walk* or the *Jolly Postman's* route.

Art and Design

- Design and make a holder to keep a map dry on a walk. Which materials would work best? How would it be carried?

- Use the idea of meandering lines like rivers, roads and contours on a map, to make collage or mixed-media patterns in blue, red and brown.

- Ask the children to re-create an interesting section of a map as a painting, for example mountainous terrain, a coastal area or dense woodland.

Tickets

Getting Started

Ask the children to bring in to school as many different kinds of tickets as they can. Talk about the sorts of venues and times when tickets are issued – for travelling, getting into concerts and sports events, at the delicatessen counter in the supermarket, to raise money (raffle tickets) and so on. You may want to establish the difference between a ticket and a receipt.

English

- Share books about journeys with the children such as *The Train Ride* by June Crebbin (Walker Books). This book has an excellent rhythm and helps the children to join in with the story. *Jazeera's Journey* by Lisa Bruce (Mammoth) will help to focus on feelings and letter writing during periods away from family and friends.

- Role-play ticket-seller and customer at the bus/railway station, or at a concert booking office. Help the children to decide what the customer needs to know and how to ask suitable questions politely. What details does the ticket-seller need to have from the customer? For example: When do they wish to travel? Do they want front or back seats? How are they paying? Do they need any special facilities such as wheelchair access?

- Read together some of the words on the tickets in your collection, and make a list of 'ticket vocabulary', for example: from, return, admit, gate, row, seat. Is all the print the same size? Why are some of the words smaller, bigger or bolder than others? Is there any writing on the back of the ticket?

- What other words can the children think of that have the 'ck' phoneme in them? Wicket, back, sack, clock? You could use these words in a class poem with a clickety clack refrain.

- Let the children – in groups or individually – choose a particular kind of ticket from the display collection. Ask them to create a story around it. Try: a lucky raffle ticket, an aeroplane ticket or a lost property ticket.

Mathematics

- Choose tickets which show numbers, for example cloakroom tickets or tickets from a delicatessen counter. Which is the highest/lowest number? Can children order them from the lowest to the highest? Add the numbers together to find the total. Which are the even/odd numbers? With younger children use only one or two tickets showing single digits, and with older or more able children use tickets with two- or three-digit numbers.

- With the children sitting in a circle, use numbered tickets to practise counting on and back. Each child in the circle says the next number in the sequence.

- Set problem-solving challenges using the prices shown on bus and train tickets. Look at the cost of a ticket and round it up or down to the nearest hundred or ten. Calculate the cost of two or more tickets. What is the most/least expensive ticket in your collection?

Information and Communication Technology

- Use a word processor to make a larger version of your class poem. Print out and illustrate the poem or jingle to make a wall frieze. You could make this into a 'Poetry on the move' poster to cheer up passengers on their train journeys to work. Try sending an e-mail or a fax of your poems and suggestions to your local train operators.

- Try story-boarding using a computer. Retell a story with a journey theme such as *Mr Gumpy's Outing* by John Burningham (Puffin Books) or use the children's own extended writing.

- Use a geography or encyclopaedia software program or a CD-ROM to find out more about some of the places shown on your ticket collection.

- Use a computer to design tickets, perhaps for a holiday flight, or tickets for a special event such as a school visit or concert (see photograph, above).

Humanities

- Plot where your tickets have come from on an enlarged local or world map. You could plot the cinema, museum, supermarket, or foreign countries visited.

- Where is your nearest airport, railway or bus station? How far is it from school? What is the quickest/easiest way to get there – rail, coach, car? Make your findings into a handy travel guide for local people.

Art and Design

- Use some of your tickets to make a large wall frieze or collage of a mode of transport. You could give it a historical perspective such as a steam train (see display photograph on page 58) or try a space travel theme.

- Design and make a card wallet for rail or air tickets. How will you stop the tickets falling out?

Flags

Getting Started

Show the children at least one flag as a starting point, or use a book of flags to generate discussion. Talk about where they may have seen flags, for example on buildings or ships, as decoration, on sandcastles at the seaside or on a sports field. Encourage them to bring in flags they may have at home to build into a display.

English

- Explore the 'fl' sound at the beginning of 'flag'. Brainstorm other words that begin with the same sound: flip, flap, flutter, flower, fly, flick. Display this word bank on a large flag outline shape and add it to your display.

- Have fun with the onomatopoeic quality of many of the words that begin with the 'fl' sound. Try writing a poem with a 'flip, flap, flutter flags in the breeze' refrain.

- Look at and discuss some of the emblems used on flags, for example dragons, stars, trees and birds. Can the children suggest ideas about why these emblems may have been used? Explore imaginative options and ideas and create stories or poetry around them.

- Working in pairs, one child can try to describe either verbally or in writing a particular flag so that their partner can draw it.

Mathematics

- Investigate the different shapes on flags, and chart the ones you have found.

- Survey which colours are most often used on flags. You could restrict this to the flags in your collection or extend the range by using European, state or world flags. Which colours are rarely or never used on flags?

- Investigate and record which flag designs have lines of symmetry.

- Make a set of number flags to decorate a sandcastle. Set the challenges and constraints according to age and ability, for example the flags must only add up to 10, 20, 30 or use three digits.

Information and Communication Technology

- Use a computer to design some flags for an imaginary land. You could use simple shapes or symbols that can be imported from a painting or drawing program or practise drawing basic shapes with the mouse, enlarging and printing them out to use on paper flags.

- Use encyclopaedia software or the Internet to find out more about some of the countries represented by the flags in your collection. Find out about the flags of world organisations such as international aid agencies, the European Union or the Commonwealth of Independent States.

Humanities

- Design a new and colourful flag for your town, village or city. Which geographical features might be included – a stream, hills, a railway station, industrial chimneys? Take the children out to look at the key geographical features of your locality. Make sketches and notes of your ideas and use these to create a new flag (see display photograph, above).

- On a world map, match flags with their countries. Make small paper flags and attach them to straws or cocktail sticks with a Plasticine base. Draw lines or use card strip arrows to connect flags to countries.

- Research other purposes for flags, for example in semaphore, to indicate surrender during a battle, to mark a new territory (such as reaching the North Pole) and the special flags used by the Red Cross and Red Crescent aid agencies. Collate the information into a reusable classroom resource such as a 'Flags Fact Pack'.

Art and Design

- Design and make flags to represent the qualities and characteristics of your school. Consider the most suitable materials and techniques to use and how the flag will be attached to its pole. How can it be rolled up?

- Use Plasticine, clay or stiff card to make 3D printing blocks using the shapes often found on flags, for example stars, crosses, crowns or suns. Use these to print designs on an old white pillow case or cut-up sheet to make your own flag drape.

- Use brightly coloured, or flourescent paper to make triangles or other interesting shapes. String the shapes together to make decorative bunting for a special occasion at school, such as a summer fair or celebration.

- Explode some of the shapes used on flags, for example circles, crosses, crescent moons and stars (see illustration, right).

Exploded flag shapes

Photographs

Getting Started

Show the children an interesting photograph – perhaps of a fascinating character, a trades person from the past doing their job, or a particularly interesting building.

On what kind of occasions do people tend to take pictures? Ask the children if they can bring some photographs or albums into school to display for a couple of weeks.

English

- Look closely at some of the characters in your photographs. What might the people be saying or thinking? Write your ideas in speech or thought bubbles and add them to the photographs. You could also use photographs from newspapers and magazines to add a topical dimension to this activity.

- Write captions for your photographs and collate them into an album or large wall frieze.

- Tell or write the story behind a photograph.

- Put together two or three characters from different photographs or use a photograph of a group scene. Work out a short sketch or role-play the characters. Try writing some scripts.

Mathematics

- Sort and classify some of the photographs into sets: people, animals, holidays.

- Rolls of film usually have 12, 24, or 36 shots. Ask the children to identify and continue the number pattern.

- Measure the dimensions of different photographs. Ask the children to put them in size order. Which is the tallest, widest or smallest photograph? What would the measurements be if you decided to have a certain photograph enlarged by 10 centimetres all round, 5 centimetres in width only, or enlarged to twice its original size?

Information and Communication Technology

- Give the children the opportunity to take photographs, perhaps with their own cameras brought in from home for the day, or a disposable one. Try making a class album of a school or local event, such as a fête or sports day.

- Help the children to make a short video film. The subject matter could be the photographs topic itself with the children preparing presentations of their work, or you could make a video of a school trip. The children should get involved with the editing and provide a commentary. Invite parents or another class to share your video.

Humanities

- Ask the children to bring in photographs of themselves taken at different stages in their lives. Arrange them in a timeline sequence and write captions (see display photograph, above).

- Look carefully at photographs taken in the past, not necessarily from the distant past – parents or grandparents as children are fine. What evidence is there in the photographs to show how things have changed? Look at clothes, transport, shop signs and so on. Annotate the pictures with your observations.

- Go out with a camera into the local environment and collect photographic evidence of its history. Take pictures of, for example the church, village or town signs, road names with a historical origin, buildings with clues to their previous use (the Old Forge, or brewery house). Use the developed photographs to illustrate a short guide to your locality.

Art and Design

- Make frames for your photographs. Try: a card with a central shape cut out, decorating the lid of a box and sticking the photograph inside it, or embellishing a photograph with a decorative border.

- Look at and assess different styles of photograph album. Ask the children to make their own photograph album. Consider how the photographs will be attached. How will they stay clean? How will the pages be held together – with staples, stitches, glue? Decorate the front cover and add some lettering.

- Cut up unwanted photographs and reassemble the pieces to make new, amusing or abstract montages, for example futuristic vehicles, funny characters or weird inventions.

- Cut up photographs and space out the pieces to make 'exploded' pictures.

Coverings

Getting Started

Brainstorm the things that are used in and around the home to cover surfaces such as floors, walls, windows, tables and furnishings. You could also look at pictures from magazines or DIY catalogues. Ask the children to bring into school any unwanted samples of material, wallpaper off-cuts, tiles and so on from home to build into a display.

English

- Consider the idea of a magic carpet. Think about other coverings from your collection which could contain magical powers, such as a magical duvet cover that takes you on fantastic dream journeys. Write a story about your own magical covering and describe where you would like it to take you. Would it be a real country or an imaginary land? What amazing things would you see on the way?

- Describe, in a word and picture sequence, how to put on a clean pillow slip or duvet cover.

- Use your coverings collection to expand the children's descriptive vocabulary. Ask them to take turns to describe a chosen covering so that others can identify it, without first knowing which piece has been picked.

Mathematics

- Become floor designers. Give the children 12 red and 12 green 'tiles' (use squares of coloured paper, or card). How many different patterns can they make? Can they record their designs on squared paper? What other patterns can they make if 3 yellow tiles are introduced?

- Use card or coloured paper tiles to work out areas. If each of the tiles used to make patterns measures 10 square centimetres, what area will the tiles cover altogether?

- Look at coverings that use a regular, tessellating pattern, such as curtain fabrics, floor coverings or tiles. Make some tessellating patterns of your own using squares, equilateral triangles or hexagons. Try tessellation with other shapes.

Information and Communication Technology

- Use a word processor to make labels and captions for the different sorts of coverings you have collected. These could be simple one- or two-word titles, or short descriptions. Try different font sizes and styles (see display photograph, above).

- Create designs for curtains or duvet covers for your own bedroom. The children could draw their basic design first on paper, then use the mouse to draw it on screen before using the copy and paste facility to make a whole page of the repeated pattern.

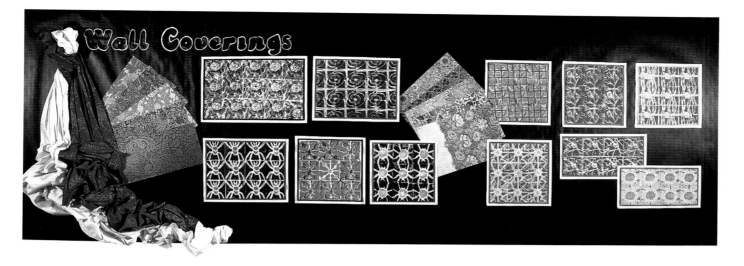

Science

- Identify and chart the different types of materials we use in the kitchen to cover leftover food (polythene food wrap, foil, greaseproof paper, plastic bags, parchment). Devise a fair test to find out which of these coverings keeps a piece of bread fresh for longest.

- Ask the children to conduct a survey around school or home of coverings used for particular purposes, for example floor, window, wall coverings, water tank jackets, roof tiles and so on. How much difference do these coverings actually make? Try an experiment of your own with water containers wrapped in a range of materials to find the best insulation covering. Was it a fair test?

Art and Design

- Work in groups to make a sample book to help somebody choose the right materials for their bedroom soft furnishings. Use small pieces of material, tile designs and wallpaper from your collection, or create completely new colour co-ordinating ranges of your own. How will the book be held together – stitches, staples or a cardboard spine binder?

- Look at wallpaper designs by William Morris. Ask the children to print some similar designs of their own. They could draw their designs on paper first. Use printing ink and polystyrene tiles to make a repeated pattern – decide which colour to leave as the base colour and overprint two or three times with different colours to make a repeated pattern (see photographs, above and right).

- Design and make a dust-jacket, with wallpaper or fabric, to protect a favourite book.

Foods from around the World

The menu in the image reads:

> ✡ Passover Menu ✡
>
> Roasted Shankbone
> Roasted egg
> Maror (bitter herbs)
> Green herbs (parsley or cress)
> Charoset (apples, nuts,
> cinnamon and wine)
> Lettuce
> Matzot (unleavened bread)
> Salted water
> Wine

Getting Started

What do the children know about food from different countries? Talk about restaurants and take-away food outlets in the local area. Collect menus and look at the types of meals on offer. From which countries do these foods originate? Talk about Indian, Chinese, Italian, Mexican, Greek and Thai foods. As a stimulus to discussion, collect packets (or wrappings) of rice, pasta, cheeses, pitta or naan bread, grains and pulses. If possible, collect some cooking utensils and equipment with an international feel, such as a wok, rice steamer and balti dish. Capitalise on the range of cultures you may have in your class, school or local community.

English

- Brainstorm and list words associated with eating, such as chew, bite, gobble, slurp. Help the children to arrange your word bank into alphabetical order and add it to your display.

- Compile recipes brought from home into a 'World Foods Recipe Book'. Alternatively, you could use the recipes to make a 'Foods of the World' calendar as a present. This could feature one country or recipe per month.

- Ask the children to select a meal from the class recipe book and write out a shopping list for the ingredients.

- Plan some menus for a celebration. What foods are eaten during Diwali, Hanukkah or the Chinese New Year, for example? The children could write their menu suggestions on specially decorated cards (see photograph, above).

- Transform a corner of the classroom into a restaurant. Ask the children to make menu signs and a specials board. Make notepads on which orders can be taken.

- Develop research skills by asking the children to research a traditional food from a country of their own choice using reference books. Examples might include spaghetti bolognese from Italy or kebabs from Greece. The children can model the food and add labels (see display photograph, page 67).

Mathematics

- Pick up handfuls of dry foods, for example pasta, pulses and rice. Estimate which handfuls weigh the most/least. How close was your estimate to the actual weight? Chart the results.

- Use menus from take-away restaurants to solve number problems involving money. For example, how much would it cost for you and a friend to have a main meal? How much if you added a side dish?

- Look at the sell-by dates on items such as rice, pasta and lentils. Chart how much time there is left between the current date and when they should be used. Record the time in months, weeks and days.

- Work out a recipe for eight people by doubling or halving quantities in a simple recipe for four people.

Information and Communication Technology

- Make a database of restaurants and take-away food outlets in your local area. Discuss with the children which fields it would be useful to have, for example name, address, telephone number and type of restaurant.

- Help the children to send an e-mail or fax message to the manager of your local supermarket asking if you can arrange a visit to find out more about where different foods come from.

Science

- Identify some of the collective nouns we use to classify food, for example fruit, vegetables, meat, fish, fats, starches and sugars. Classify samples of your international food collection (or their packets) into appropriate sets.

- Introduce the idea of groups of foods for particular purposes, such as growth or energy.

- Invite a vegetarian or Indian cook into school to discuss their diet and to explain how they ensure that they have a balanced intake of different food types. Alternatively, present the children with a collection of foods from a range of cultures and discuss how they can be combined for a healthy diet.

Humanities

- Visit a local supermarket to find out where foods come from. Plot the foods and countries of origin on a world map.

- Investigate the links between food production and climate. Find out which foods are grown in hot tropical climates and which are grown in temperate and cold zones, and compare them.

Art and Design

- Invite community cooks, such as parents, a chef or baker into school to give a cookery demonstration and work alongside groups of children to make a speciality dish. Enjoy the tasting session.
  Safety note: Check for food allergies/special diets.

- Design a front cover for a menu of a restaurant specialising in food from a particular country.

Packaging

Getting Started

Begin by making a collection of cartons, empty packets and food wrappers. Look at these more closely with the children and establish that they are all forms of packaging. Look at and discuss the wrappings in the children's lunch boxes. Broaden the discussion to include packaging on new clothes and household, office and school goods. Ask each of the children to bring in some packaging to build into a display.

Note: Make sure the packaging is clean. Children should wash their hands after handling food wrappers.

English

- Share books on the theme of packaging, recycling and waste, for example *Professor Noah's Spaceship* by Brian Wildsmith (Oxford University Press), *Dinosaurs and All that Rubbish* by Michael Foreman (Puffin Books), *Charlie's House* by Reviva Schermbrucker (Oxford University Press), *Toby's Doll's House* by Ragnhild Scamell (David and Charles Children's Books). Encourage the children to consider how packaging and waste materials feature in the stories. What are the main messages? What items have the children recycled, and how do they feel about seeing litter and rubbish in the environment?

- Use packaging as a stimulus for shared reading activities. Read all the words on a cereal packet with the children. Talk about the different forms of writing used, such as the name of the product and brand, description of contents, list of ingredients, nutritional information, recipe suggestions and sell-by dates.

- Identify initial sounds and blends in the words on packaging (<u>m</u>ilk, <u>c</u>risps, etc.). Have fun making up new, alliterative names with the initial sounds you have found, perhaps matched up to a child's name (for example Milky Mary, Orangey Oliver). What might some of these invented characters look like?

- Write a letter to a company suggesting improvements to a particular product's packaging (new colours, image or environmentally friendly materials and advice).

- Make up a cartoon strip, short story or narrative poem about 'the carton that just couldn't be emptied'.

Mathematics

- Open up a variety of boxes and cartons to investigate nets. Make similar nets on squared paper, a peg board or with polyhedrons or geostrips.

- Make a montage from sweet wrappers. Use squared paper to replicate the montage design. Now try enlarging the design by using more squares per section (see photograph, below).

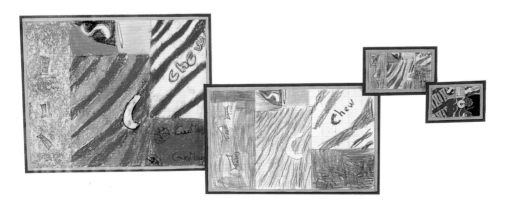

- Investigate the dimensions of cartons and boxes from your collection. How many sides or faces do they have? How tall are they? What are the differences in length between the longest and shortest sides? Can the children order the cartons and boxes from the tallest to the shortest?

- Survey recycling practices. Ask the children to find out from home if they recycle newspapers, cans, bottles, clothes and so on. Collate the data and show as a picture graph or bar chart. Which form of packaging do most/fewest people recycle?

Information and Communication Technology

- Encourage the children to use a computer to make their own simple worksheets to record the nouns, verbs and adjectives (or different forms of writing such as lists, titles, addresses) found on packaging. Some children may, with help, be able to insert a three-column table to record these different parts of speech.

- Use a computer to design and print out large recycling notices to be displayed around school to promote recycling, for example: 'Please recycle your cans in our can bank' and 'Don't just bin it – recycle it'.

Science

- Ask the children to name and describe the properties of materials used in various types of packaging: plastic, glass, paper, hard, bendy, waterproof, and so on. Investigate ways of sorting and classifying your packaging collection.

- Can the children describe a packaging material from your collection, using terms such as transparent, flexible and strong, so that others can identify it?

- Look at the different types of packaging in your collection and ask the children why each material was used to make the object and give reasons why it is suitable. Consider why packaging might have to keep out the light, be water-tight, air-tight and light in weight. Ask the children to chart their ideas, and display them with your collection.

- Have fun making boats from plastic bottles to sail across the water-tray or sink. Try making rafts by joining bottles together. Can the children devise a test to work out how to sink the boats or rafts? Older or more able children can investigate ways of powering their boats (by using elastic bands or creating draughts, for example).

Humanities

- Investigate what happens to waste packaging when we put it in the dustbin. As well as researching from books and computers, write to manufacturers asking for any information they may have on their packaging companies. Compile the findings into a 'Did You Know?' card, perhaps focusing on the four Rs: Reduce, Reuse, Recover and Recycle.

- Make up symbols to mark local recycling centres on a simple map of your locality, or map the litter bins, can banks and so on in and around your school.

- Research the history of manufactured materials often used in packaging, such as plastic, polystyrene foam and nylon thread. What did we use before they were invented?

- Invite a retired shopkeeper or older member of the community into school to talk to the children about how shopkeepers used to weigh out and distribute their products. How did customers carry their shopping home? What effect do the children think supermarkets have had on shopping, packaging and waste?

Art and Design

- Make large masks incorporating waste materials, like the Greek gods in the photograph above.

- Use wrappers as a stimulus to sew 3D sweet packaging (see photograph, below).

- Use brightly coloured food wrappings to make letters for your display (see display photograph on page 69).

- Look at barcodes on packaging. Make some abstract designs in black and white using, for example, paint, ink, charcoal and felt-tip pens. Encourage the children to look carefully at the widths and positions of the lines. Try 'exploding' the patterns by leaving bigger white spaces or making thicker lines. What sorts of patterns can be made by adding diagonal or horizontal lines? You could go on to make barcode prints from polystyrene tiles and black ink or thick paint, or by using the edges of card or wood.